A SCHOOL HISTORY OF THE GREAT WAR

A SCHOOL HISTORY OF THE GREAT WAR

By

ALBERT E. McKINLEY, PH.D.

CHARLES A. COULOMB, PH.D.

AND

ARMAND J. GERSON, PH.D.

GYAN

Published by

Gyan Publishing House
5, Ansari Road
Daryaganj, New Delhi-110002
Phone: 011-47034999, 9811692060
E-mail: books@gyanbooks.com

Distribution Network
gyanbooks.com
India, USA, Canada, UK, Australia, France

ISBN : 978-81-212-6428-0 (PB)
First Published, 1918

2nd Impression 2022

Printed at: Gyan Press, Delhi.

A SCHOOL HISTORY OF THE GREAT WAR
Author: **ALBERT E. McKINLEY**

A SCHOOL HISTORY OF THE GREAT WAR

BY

ALBERT E. McKINLEY, Ph.D.

CHARLES A. COULOMB, Ph.D.

AND

ARMAND J. GERSON, Ph.D.

PREFACE

THIS brief history of the world's greatest war was prepared upon the suggestion of the National Board for Historical Service. Its purpose is to expand into an historical narrative the outline of the study of the war which the authors prepared for the Board and which was published by the United States Bureau of Education as Teachers' Leaflet No. 4, in August, 1918. The arrangement of chapters and the choice of topics have been largely determined by the various headings in the outline for the course in grades seven and eight.

The authors trust that the simple presentation here given may aid in developing a national comprehension of the issues involved in the war; and they hope it may play some part in preparing the American people for the solution of the great problems which lie immediately before us.

CONTENTS

A School History of the Great War

CHAPTER I

EUROPE BEFORE THE GREAT WAR

To understand the Great War it is not sufficient to read the daily happenings of military and naval events as they are told in newspapers and magazines. We must go back of the facts of to-day and find in national history and personal ambition the causes of the present struggle. Years of preparation were necessary before German military leaders could convert a nation to their views, or get ready the men, munitions, and transportation for the war they wanted. Conflicts of races for hundreds of years have made the southeastern part of Europe a firebrand in international affairs. The course of the Russian revolution has been determined largely by the history of the Russian people and of the Russian rulers during the past two centuries. The entrance of England and Italy into the war against Germany was in each case brought about by causes which came into existence long before August, 1914. A person who understands, even in part, the causes of

EUROPE in 1913
SCALE OF MILES
0 100 200 300 400 500
ATLANTIC OCEAN
NORTH SEA
BALTIC SEA
MEDITERRANEAN SEA
ADRIATIC SEA
AEGEAN SEA
BLACK SEA
NORWAY
SWEDEN
FINLAND
DENMARK
GREAT BRITAIN
SCOTLAND
IRELAND
WALES
ENGLAND
HOLLAND
BELGIUM
GERMAN EMPIRE
FRANCE
SWITZ.
SPAIN
PORTUGAL
ITALY
AUSTRIA HUNGARY
BOHEMIA
RUSSIA
POLAND
ROUMANIA
SERBIA
BULGARIA
MON.
ALBANIA
GREECE
TURKISH EMPIRE
ASIA
CAUCASUS
MOROCCO
ALGERIA
TUNIS
CORSICA
SARDINIA
SICILY
HELGOLAND
Kiel Canal
Christiania
Stockholm
St. Petersburg
Moscow
Copenhagen
Dublin
London
The Hague
Rotterdam
Antwerp
Brussels
Havre
Paris
Luxemburg
Berlin
Warsaw
Vienna
Budapest
Bern
Bordeaux
Venice
Trieste
Belgrade
Bucharest
Sofia
Adrianople
Constantinople
Salonica
Athens
Odessa
Lisbon
Madrid
Gibraltar
Rome
Rhine
Danube R.
Dnieper R.
Volga R.
9

this great struggle, will be in a better position to realize why America entered the war and what our nation is fighting for. And better yet, he will be more ready to take part in settling the many problems of peace which must come after the war is over. For these reasons, the first few chapters of this book are devoted to a study of the important facts of recent European history.

A Hundred Years Ago. — It is remarkable that almost exactly a century before the present world war, Europe was engaged in a somewhat similar struggle to prevent an ambitious French general, Napoleon Bonaparte, from becoming the ruler of all that continent, and of America as well. He had conquered or intimidated nearly all the states of Europe — Austria, Prussia, Russia, Spain, etc. — except Great Britain. He once planned a great settlement on the Mississippi River, and so alarmed President Jefferson that the latter said the United States might be compelled to "marry themselves to the British fleet and nation." But England's navy kept control of the seas; Napoleon's colony in North America was never founded; and at last the peoples of Europe rose against their conqueror, and in the battle of Waterloo, June 18, 1815, finally overthrew him.

Europe Since 1815. — After the downfall of Napoleon the rulers of Europe met in conference at Vienna and sought to restore conditions as they had been before the war. They were particularly anxious that the great masses of the people in their several nations should continue to respect what was termed "the divine right of kings to rule over their subjects." They did not, except in Great Britain, believe in representative governments. They feared free speech and independent newspapers and liberal educational institutions. They hated all kinds of popular movements by which the inhabitants of any country might throw off the monarch's yoke and secure a share in their own government. For over thirty years the "Holy Allies," — the name applied to the monarchs of Austria, Prussia, and Russia, — succeeded tolerably well in keeping the peoples in subjection. But they had many difficulties to face, and after 1848 their policy was largely given up.

Democratic Movements. — During the nineteenth century the people of Europe were restive under the rule of kings, and gradually governments controlled in greater or less degree by the people were established. Almost every decade saw popular uprisings in some of the European states. About 1820 insurrections occurred in Greece, in Spain, and in southern Italy; and the Spanish American colonies revolted from the mother country. In 1830 popular uprisings took place in France, Belgium, Germany, Poland, and other places. In 1848 a far more serious movement occurred, which overthrew the French monarchy and established a republic. From France the flame of liberty lighted fires of insurrection in Germany, Austria, Poland, and Italy. Similar attempts were made at later times. As a result of these popular uprisings and of the growing education of all classes of the people, manhood suffrage and representative institutions were established in most of the European states.

National Aspirations. — The Holy Allies had refused to recognize the right of nations to independent existence. They had bartered peoples and provinces "as if they were chattels and pawns in a game." But when the peoples tried to found democratic governments, they often discovered that the quickest and surest way was to unite under one government all who belonged to a given nationality. Thus the last hundred years in Europe has witnessed the erection of a number of new national states created by throwing off the yoke of some foreign ruler. Among the new nations thus established were (1) Belgium, freed from the kingdom of Holland; (2) Greece, Serbia, Roumania, Bulgaria, and Albania, freed from Turkish rule; (3) Italy, united out of territories controlled by petty sovereigns and Austrian rulers; (4) Norway, separated from Sweden. The same period saw also the unification of a number of German states into the German Empire. But during this time several races were unsuccessful in obtaining independence, among which we may note the Poles (in Russia, Prussia, and Austria), the Czechs (checks), or Bohemians (in northern Austria), the Finns (in the northwestern part of the Russian Empire), and the Slavic people in the southern part of Austria-Hungary.

Industrial Development. — The nineteenth century was not only a period of political change in Europe. It was also a time of great changes in the general welfare of the people. It witnessed a remarkable alteration in everyday employments and habits. In 1800 a great part of the population was engaged in agriculture. Manufacturing and commerce were looked upon as of minor importance. The goods that were produced were made by hand labor in the workman's own home. Beginning first in England about 1750 and extending to the Continent between 1820 and 1860, there came a great industrial change. The steam engine was applied to spinning, weaving, and countless other operations which previously had been performed by hand. Steam engines could not of course be installed in every small cottage; hence a number of machines were put in one factory to be run by one steam engine. The workers left their small huts and gardens in the country and came to live in towns and cities. After the steam engine came steam transportation on land and water. Then followed an enormous demand for coal, iron, steel, and other metals. More goods could be produced in the factories than were needed for the people at home. Hence arose more extended commerce and the search for foreign markets.

Colonial Expansion. — In the sixteenth and seventeenth centuries, Spain, Portugal, France, and England settled the American continents and parts of Asia. By a series of wars in the seventeenth and eighteenth centuries the Dutch secured part of the possessions of Spain and Portugal; and England obtained almost all of the French colonial territories. In the eighteenth century the thirteen English colonies on the Atlantic seaboard made good their independence; and in the nineteenth, Spain lost all of her vast possessions in America. During the early nineteenth century, Great Britain, in spite of the loss of the thirteen colonies, was by far the most successful colonizing country, and her possessions were to be found in Canada, India, the East and West Indies, Australia, and Africa.

Leaders of other nations in Europe thought these colonies of Great Britain were the cause of her wealth and prosperity. Naturally they too tried to found colonies in those parts of the world not occupied by Europeans. They hoped by this means to extend their power, to find homes for their surplus population, and to obtain markets for their new manufactured goods. Thus Africa was parceled out among France, Germany, Great Britain, Portugal, Belgium, Spain, and Italy. The islands of the Pacific were seized in the same manner. Proposals for a partition of China were made by Germany, Russia, Japan, France, and Great Britain; and if it it had not been for the American demands for the "open door of trade" and for the "territorial integrity" of China, that nation probably would have shared the fate of Africa. The noteworthy fact about this rivalry for colonies is that almost the entire world, except China and Japan, came under the domination of Europeans and their descendants.

Having noted a few general features of European

history during the nineteenth century, we shall now take up in turn each of the more important countries.

Germany. — After the overthrow of Napoleon, a German Confederation was formed. This comprised thirty-nine states which were bound to each other by a very weak tie. The union was not so strong even as that in our own country under the Articles of Confederation. But there were two states in the German Confederation which were far stronger than any of the others; these were Austria and Prussia. Austria had been a great power in German and European affairs for centuries; but her rulers were now incompetent and corrupt. Prussia, on the other hand, was an upstart, whose strength lay in universal military service. As the century progressed, the influence of Prussia became greater; and the jealousy of Austria grew proportionately. Bismarck, the Prussian prime minister, adopted a policy of "blood and iron." By this he meant that Prussia would attain the objects of her ambition by means of war. Under his guidance she would intimidate or conquer the other German states and force them into trade and commercial agreements, or annex their territory to that of Prussia.

Bismarck looked for success only to the army. With the king back of him, he defied the people's representatives, ignored the Prussian constitution, and purposely picked quarrels with his neighbors. In 1866, in a brief war of seven weeks, Austria was hopelessly defeated and forced to retire from the German Confederation.

In 1870, when he felt sure of his military preparations, Bismarck altered a telegram and thus brought on a war with France. The Franco-Prussian War lasted only a few months; but in that time the French were thoroughly defeated. Many important results followed the war: (1) The German states, influenced by the patriotic excitement of a successful war, founded the German Empire, with Prussia in the leading position, and the Prussian king as German emperor or "Kaiser." (2) A huge indemnity of one billion dollars was exacted by Prussia from France, and this money, deposited in the German banks and loaned to individuals, played a large part in expanding the manufactures and commerce of Germany. (3) Prussia took away from France, against the wishes of the inhabitants, the provinces called Alsace-Lorraine. This "wrong done to France," as President Wilson has said, "unsettled the peace of the world for nearly fifty years." (4) The French people carried through a revolution and established a republic — for the third time in their history — which has continued down to the present.

After 1870 Germany made remarkable material progress. By 1911 her population had grown from 41,000,000 to 65,000,000. Her coal and iron production in 1911 was eight times as much as in 1871. In wealth, commerce, coal production, and textile industries, among European countries, Germany was second only to Great Britain; while in the production of iron and steel Germany had passed Great Britain and was second only to the United States.

But this great industrial and commercial advance was not accompanied with a corresponding liberality in government. The constitution of the German Empire gave very large powers to the emperor, and very little power to the representatives of the people. Prussia, the dominant state in the empire, had an antiquated system of voting which rated men's votes according to the taxes they paid, and placed political power in the hands of a small number of capitalists and wealthy landowners, especially the Junkers (yoong'kerz), or Prussian nobles. The educational system, while giving a rudimentary education to all, was really designed to keep large masses of the people subject to the military group, the government officials, and the capitalists. Blind devotion to the emperor and belief in the necessity of future war in order to increase German prosperity, were widely taught. The "mailed fist" was clenched, and "the shining sword" rattled in the scabbard whenever Germany thought the other nations of Europe showed her a lack of respect. Enormous preparations for war were made in order that Germany might gain from her neighbors the "place in the sun" which she was determined upon. Other nations were to be pushed aside or be broken to pieces in order that the German "super-men" might enjoy all that they wished of this world's goods and possessions.

Austria-Hungary. — The Austro-Hungarian Monarchy in 1910 had a population of 49,000,000, made up of peoples and races who spoke different languages and had different customs, habits, and ideals. These races, instead of being brought under unifying influences as foreigners are in the United States, had for centuries retained their peculiarities. Germans comprised 24 per cent of the total population; Hungarians, 20 per cent; Slavic races (including Bohemians, Poles, South Slavs, and others), 45 per cent; Roumanians, over 6 per cent; and Italians less than 2 per cent. The Germans and Hungarians, although only a minority of the total population, had long exercised political control over the others and by repressive measures had tried to stamp out their schools, newspapers, and languages. Unrest was continuous during the nineteenth century; and the rise of the independent states of Serbia, Roumania, and Bulgaria tended to make the Slavic and Roumanian inhabitants of Austria-Hungary dissatisfied with their own position.

After 1815 the Austro-Hungarian Monarchy continued under the rule of the royal family of Hapsburgs, whose proud history extends back to the fifteenth century. Austria (but not Hungary) was part of the German Confederation, and her representative had the right of presiding at all meetings of the confederation. Between 1815 and 1848 the Austrian emperor and his prime minister were the leaders in opposition to popular government and national aspirations. But in 1848 a serious uprising took place, and it seemed for a time that the diverse peoples would fly apart from each other and establish separate states. The emperor abdicated and his prime minister fled to England. Francis Joseph, the young heir to the throne, with the aid of experienced military leaders succeeded in suppressing the rebellion. For sixty-eight years (1848–1916) he was personally popular and held together the composite state.

In 1866 Austria was driven out of the German Confederation by Prussia. Seven years earlier she had lost most of her Italian possessions. Thereafter her interests and ambitions lay to the southeast; and she bent her energies to extend her territory, influence, and commerce into the Balkan region. A semblance of popular government was established in Austria and in Hungary, which were separated from each other in ordinary affairs, but continued under the same monarch. In each country, however, the suffrage and elections were so juggled that the ruling minority, of Germans in Austria and of Hungarians in Hungary, was enabled to keep the majority in subjection.

Austria-Hungary has not progressed as rapidly in industry and commerce as the countries to the north and west of her. Her life is still largely agricultural, and cultivation is often conducted by primitive methods. Before the war her wealth per person was only $500, as compared with $1843 in the United States, $1849 in Great Britain, $1250 in France, and $1230 in Germany. She possessed only one good seaport, Trieste (trĭ-ĕst′), and this partly explained her desire to obtain access to the Black Sea and the Ægean Sea. About half of her foreign trade was carried on with Germany. The low standards of national wealth and production made the raising of taxes a difficult matter. The government had a serious struggle to obtain the funds for a large military and naval program.

Italy. — For a thousand years before 1870 there was no single government for the entire Italian peninsula. Although the people were mainly of one race, their territory was divided into small states ruled by despotic princes, who were sometimes of Italian families, but more often were foreigners — Greeks, Germans, French, Spanish, and Austrians. The Pope, head of the Roman Catholic Church, governed nearly one third of the land. This condition continued after 1815. But during the nineteenth century the Italians began to realize that they belonged to one race. They saw that the rule of foreigners was opposed to the national welfare.

By 1870 the union of all Italy into one kingdom was completed. In this work three great men participated, as well as many lesser patriots. The first was Garibal′di, a man of intense courage and patriotism. He aroused the young men of Italy to the need of national union and the expulsion of the foreigners. For over thirty years he was engaged in various military expeditions which aided greatly in the establishment of the national union. The second leader was of an entirely different character. Count Cavour (ka-voor′) was a statesman, a politician, a deep student of European history, and a man of great tact. He, too, wished for a united Italy, but he believed union could not be gained without foreign assistance. By most skillful means he secured the support of France and of England, while at the same time he used Garibaldi and his revolutionists. He had succeeded, at the time of his death in 1861, in bringing together all of Italy except Rome and Venice. He won for the new Italian kingdom a place among the great nations of Europe.

The third great Italian was Victor Emman′uel, king of Sardinia. He approved of a limited monarchy, like that of England, instead of the corrupt despotisms which existed in most of the Italian peninsula. He knew how to use men like Cavour and Garibaldi to achieve the national ambitions. By a popular vote in each part of Italy Victor Emmanuel was accepted as king of the united nation. The country was not ready for a republic; but Victor Emmanuel proved a wise national leader, willing to reign according to a written constitution under which the people's representatives had the determining voice in the government. In 1870 the king entered Rome and early the next year proclaimed the city to be the capital of Italy.

Belgium. — The country we now know as Belgium has had a very checkered history. At one time or another it has been controlled by German, French, Spanish, and Austrian rulers. At the opening of the nineteenth century it was annexed to the kingdom of

Holland (1815). But a revolt took place in 1830, and the Belgians separated from the Dutch and chose a king for themselves. Their constitution declares that the government is a "constitutional, representative, and hereditary monarchy." The government is largely in the control of the people or their representatives. There is one voter for every five persons in the population, nearly the same proportion as in the United States. In 1839 the principal states of Europe agreed to recognize Belgium's independence, and in case of war among themselves to treat her territory as neutral land, not to be invaded. This treaty was signed by Prussia as well as by Austria, France, Great Britain, and Russia. The treaty was again acknowledged by Prussia in 1870. It was in violation of these treaties, as we shall see, that Prussian and other German troops invaded Belgium on August 4, 1914.

France. — In 1789 France entered upon a period of revolution. The old monarchy was shortly overthrown, and with it went aristocracy and all the inequalities of the Middle Ages. A republic, however, did not long endure; and Napoleon Bonaparte used his position as a successful general to establish a new monarchy called the French Empire. After Napoleon's downfall, the allied monarchs of Europe restored the old line of kings in France. But the country had outgrown despotism. A revolution in 1830 deposed one king and set up another who was ready to rule under the terms of a constitution. In 1848 this monarchy was displaced and the second French republic was established. But again a Bonaparte, nephew of Napoleon I, seized the government and established a second empire, calling himself Napoleon III. He aped the ways of his great predecessor and tried by foreign conquest or annexation in Africa, Italy, and Mexico to dazzle the French people. But he was never popular, and his reign closed in the defeat and disgrace of the Franco-Prussian War (1870–71), for which he was partly responsible.

The third French republic was proclaimed in 1870 and is the present government of the country. Under the constitution there is a senate, the members of which are elected for nine years, and a lower house, elected for four years. The president is chosen by these two houses of the legislature for a term of seven years. No member of the old royal families may become president of the republic. The president of France does not possess nearly so much power as the president of the United States. Many of the executive duties are performed by the premier, or prime minister, and other cabinet ministers.

Republican France has become one of the great nations of the world, and its democratic institutions are firmly rooted in the hearts of the people. It has been compelled to face German militarism by erecting a system of universal military training. The patriotism and self-sacrifice of all classes during the Great War have been beyond praise.

Great Britain. — During the nineteenth century Great Britain did not experience any of the sudden revolutions which appeared in nearly every other country of Europe. For centuries England, Scotland, and Ireland had possessed representative institutions. When reforms were needed, they were adopted gradually, by the natural process of lawmaking, instead of resulting from rebellion and revolt. In this way Great Britain had been changed from an aristocratic government to one founded on democratic principles. By 1884 the suffrage was nearly as extensive as in the United States. Parliament became as truly representative of the people's will as our American Congress. Far-reaching social reforms were adopted which advanced the general welfare. Among these reforms were acts for improving housing conditions, regulating hours of labor and use of machinery in factories, and establishing a national insurance system, old-age pensions, and compensation to injured workmen.

Great Britain was the first nation to experience the advantages and disadvantages of the new age of coal and iron, and the new methods of factory production. Her wealth and commerce grew at a rapid rate, and she invested her profits in enterprises in many parts of the world. The factory system drew so many workers from the farms, that Great Britain no longer raised sufficient food for her population. She became dependent upon the United States, Australia, South America, and other lands for wheat, meat, and other necessaries of life. Her merchant vessels were to be found in all parts of the world; and her navy was increased from year to year to protect her commerce and colonies. From now on it became evident that England's existence depended upon her ships. If in time of war she lost control of the seas the enemy could starve her into submission. Hence during the nineteenth century Great Britain's policy was to maintain a fleet stronger than that of any possible combination against her.

England's colonial system had been developed into a great empire. Principles of English liberty and representative government were carried by Britishers to many parts of the world. The American Revolution showed the mother country that Englishmen would not brook oppression even by their own king and parliament. During the nineteenth and twentieth centuries England adopted the policy of erecting her colonies into self-governing communities. Thus the separate colonies in Canada, in Australia, and in South Africa were grouped in each case into a federal government, somewhat similar to that of the United States, and three great British democracies were formed within the boundaries of the empire. So successful has been the British system of colonial government that there has been virtually no question of loyalty during the Great War. All parts of the dominions have contributed in men and money to the common cause, and frequent imperial war conferences have been held in London. In these conferences representatives from the colonies and the mother country have joined in the discussion of important imperial questions.

Turkey and the Balkans. — In 1453 the Turks captured Constantinople. Thereafter their power was rapidly extended in southeastern Europe and for several centuries they were the dominant power in the Balkan peninsula. During this time they overran Hungary and invaded Austria up to the walls of Vienna. They subjugated Greece and all the lands now included in Serbia, Roumania, Bulgaria, Albania, as well as a number of near-by Austrian, Hungarian, and Russian provinces.

Many diverse races were included within the Turkish dominions. They differed among themselves in language, religion, and culture. The Turks were Mohammedans, while their subject peoples in Europe were mainly Christians belonging to the Greek Orthodox Church.

First driven out of Hungary and Russia during the eighteenth century, the Turks lost nearly all their European possessions in the nineteenth and early twentieth centuries. The subject peoples had kept their national traditions and customs and from time to time they aimed at independence. The Turkish rule was oppressive and at times its methods were barbarous. If there had been no jealousies among the great European powers, it is probable that Russia would have occupied Constantinople long ago. The other powers, fearing this might make Russia too strong, interfered on several occasions to prevent such an occupation. But the powers could not prevent the smaller nationalities from attaining their independence from Turkey. Greece, Serbia, Roumania, Bulgaria, and Albania were freed from the rule of the "unspeakable Turk" and erected into independent kingdoms at various times between 1829 and 1913. Of her great empire in Europe, Turkey retained, at the outbreak of the Great War, an area of less than 11,000 square miles (less than the area of the state of Maryland), and a population of 1,890,000, which was almost altogether resident in the two cities of Constantinople and Adrianople.

Russia. — In 1914 Russia was an empire occupying one seventh of the land area of the world and inhabited by about 180,000,000 people. During the nineteenth century the country was ruled by absolute monarchs called czars, under whom political and social conditions were corrupt and oppressive. However, some progress was made during the century. Serfdom or slavery was abolished from 1861 to 1866; restraints upon newspapers, publishers, and schools were partly withdrawn. Natural resources were developed, factories established, and railroads built. But these measures only served to whet the appetite of the people for more liberal government. The activities of revolutionists and reformers were met by most severe measures on the part of the government. Thousands were transported to Siberia and many were executed. Even as late as

1903 five thousand persons were imprisoned, exiled, or executed for political activity against the Czar's government. An attempt of the people to force a representative government upon the Czar failed after a seeming success in 1905–1906; for the Duma, or legislative assembly, then created was given little power.

Russia has not been fortunate in her relations with the neighboring states. Her great ambition, the occupation of Constantinople, was repeatedly balked by other countries. In an attempt to obtain an ice-free harbor on the Pacific, Russia brought on the Russo-Japanese War of 1904–1905, in which she was disastrously defeated. In another direction Russia was more successful. She posed as the protector of the Slavic provinces under Turkish rule and saw the day when nearly all of them were free.

Russia is a country of vast territory, enormous population, and unbounded natural resources. But before the war it had no experience in self-government. Its land and mineral resources were not used for national purposes. A small governing class, with the Czar at the head, controlled its tremendous powers and wealth. Naturally, when an insurrection is successful against such a government, the people lose all self-control and go to great extremes. Liberty and self-government succeed only when all the people are willing to abide by the laws made by the majority. May this time soon come for Russia!

Suggestions for Study. — 1. Look up facts concerning Napoleon Bonaparte, Gladstone, Bismarck, Cavour, Garibaldi, Victor Emmanuel I. 2. On outline maps of the world show the principal colonial possessions of Great Britain, France, Germany, Italy, Belgium, and Holland. 3. Show on an outline map of Europe the location of peoples that had not attained to national independence before 1914. 4. Compare the size and population of the European countries with your own state in the American Union. 5. How far did the people in European countries possess a share in their government in 1914? 6. Look up in detail the government of Germany.

References. — For facts such as those mentioned above see the *World Almanac*, the *Statesman's Yearbook*, and any good encyclopedia. For Germany, see Hazen, *The Government of Germany*, published by the Committee on Public Information, Washington, D. C.[1] Reference may also be made to Harding's *New Medieval and Modern History* or to other histories of Europe.

[1] Hereafter the publications of the Committee on Public Information are indicated as follows: (C. P. I.).

CHAPTER II

WHY GERMANY WANTED WAR

It would be impossible to make a list of all the causes which led Germany from time to time to take such action as would tend to force war on one or another of the nations of Europe. For besides questions of national honor or of national rights there were the writings of German philosophers, historians, and scientists, a great majority of whom maintained that war was a necessity if men were to continue to live in large groups or societies. These writers were chiefly Prussian, but Prussia, including more than half of Germany, dominated the rest of the empire through the organization of its government. The following paragraphs present what seem to be the chief reasons why Germany, and especially Prussia, wanted war.

War as a Profitable Business. — According to those German writers there are two results from a successful war. First, the victors take more or less territory from the vanquished; second, the victors may demand a large sum of money, called an indemnity, from the defeated people, who thus have to pay their conquerors for having taken the trouble to defeat them.

In both of these instances the result is advantageous to the winner of the war, and particularly to the governing class of that nation. Through the taxes from the new territory more money flows into the national treasury, and a great many new officials must be appointed. These, of course, for many years are appointed by the rulers of the victorious nation. Besides this not only do we find new markets opened up for the manufacturers and merchants, but the conquered territory frequently contains great stores of raw materials. In both cases the goods can now pass to and fro without the drawbacks of possible embargoes or import taxes which interfere with the freedom of trade. This is well illustrated by the results of the seizure of part of Lorraine by Germany from France in 1870. Lorraine contains great stores of coal and iron ore. These Germany wanted. So that part of Lorraine was demanded which would give to Germany rich mines of coal and iron. Some other ore deposits, which could not be easily utilized, she left to France. Not long afterwards a new process for making iron was discovered which made the French deposits more valuable than those Germany had taken. Undoubtedly one of the reasons for the present war was that Germany wished to increase her national wealth by seizing the iron mines that had become so valuable.

Many times before 1870 the Prussians had made large gains, in the way of increased territory and prestige, by means of war. It was the boast of many Prussian kings that each one of them had added to the lands over which he ruled. In almost every instance this increase was due to a successful war, enabling the king of Prussia to seize territory which did not belong to him.

The indemnity which may be collected from a conquered nation is also a source of profit to the conqueror. The money is deposited by the government in banks, which thus have large sums ready to lend to manufacturers and merchants who wish to increase their business. The result of this is a great stimulation of manufactures and commerce. In the case of Germany, the effect on industry of the $1,000,000,000 of indemnity which she received from France following the Franco-Prussian war was so great that Germany was soon manufacturing more than her people could consume, and German commercial agents spread all over the globe seeking to find profitable customers for the surplus.

On the other hand, the German leaders have failed to realize that the destruction of men and materials in war is always a great national loss. In the case of a long war, the losses from these causes may, even for the victors, overbalance any advantage which may be secured in the way of territory or money from the vanquished nation.

Germany Wanted Land from her Neighbors. — The present war was largely the result of Germany's desire to secure territory. The territory that was particularly wanted was in a number of different places.

In the first place, Germany coveted the rest of the iron mines which she had made the mistake (from her point of view) of letting France keep in 1870. These are located along the northeast frontier of France, about half a dozen miles from the boundary. Germany wanted also the greater part of Belgium, because it has valuable iron ore deposits, and especially because it has great deposits of coal. It has been said that without these mines of Belgian coal and of French iron, which Germany seized at the very beginning of the war, she would soon have had to give up the fight.

In the second place, Germany's only ports are on the shallow north coast, and the channels are intricate and difficult of navigation. These ports are inconveniently situated for exports from Germany's chief manufacturing region, the lower Rhine valley. The best ports for western Germany are Antwerp, in Belgium, and Rotterdam, in Holland. Germany wanted a port toward the west through which she could more conveniently reach her customers in North and South America and elsewhere. It is interesting to notice that the river Scheldt (skelt), on which Antwerp is situated, passes through Holland on its way to the sea. Even if Germany secured Belgium this would not give her control of the Antwerp outlet nor would it give her Rotterdam. It is certain that eventual domination of Holland was part of Germany's plan.

Germany wanted that part of Russia which was along the Baltic Sea. The part of Germany adjoining this, called East Prussia, is the stronghold of the Prussian Junkers, or landed nobility. These people already own great estates in the Baltic provinces of Russia.

Germany wished to govern this German-owned land and provide a place to which her surplus population could emigrate and still be in German territory. The Junkers were especially anxious for this to come about as it would greatly increase their power in Germany.

"Pan-Germanists" is the name given to a group of German leaders who aimed especially to bring all German-speaking peoples into the German Empire. In general, however, the same leaders aimed to bring under German control all the districts that have been mentioned above, together with the Balkan states and other lands.

Germany Wanted More Colonies. — Germany's commercial expansion came after most of the world had been divided among the other nations. She thought she must have more colonies to provide her with raw materials and to give her markets for some of her surplus manufactures. Other reasons why Germany wanted colonies were that she might obtain more food, and that she might establish coaling stations for her navy, so that it could protect her commerce, especially her food-carrying ships. As the war has shown, Germany can hardly produce a full supply of food for her own people.

The easiest way to get colonies seemed to be by making war against some nation that already possessed them, in the hope that a victorious Germany could seize the colonies she desired. On the other hand, without war, she had gained some large colonies and was assured of others in Africa, and she had secured a prevailing influence over the immense domains of Turkey in Asia. By 1914 the Germans had more than half completed a railroad through Turkey to the Persian Gulf, and expected soon to dominate the eastern trade by the Berlin-Bagdad route.

Germany Wanted "a Place in the Sun." — Germany was acknowledged to be the strongest nation in continental Europe. Her position as a world power, however, was disputed by Great Britain, both by reason of the latter's control of the sea through her enormous fleet, and by reason of Great Britain's numerous colonies all over the world. It was galling to German pride to have to coal her ships at English coaling stations. She wanted stations of her own. By bringing on a war that would humble France to the dust and make Belgium a part of Germany, thus giving her a chance to seize the colonies of France and Belgium, Germany would at once attain a position in

THE BERLIN-BAGDAD RAILWAY

the world's affairs which would enable her to challenge the power of any nation on earth.

The Survival of the Fittest. — German thinkers carried to an extreme the theory of the survival of the fittest. This doctrine teaches that all living things have reached their present forms through a gradual development of those qualities which best fit them to live in their present surroundings. Those that are best adapted live on, and produce a new generation that are also well fitted to survive. Those that are not fitted to their surroundings soon give up the struggle and die. The Germans applied this same belief to nations, and claimed that only those nations survived that could successfully meet world conditions. They believed that war was an inevitable world condition, and that that nation would survive that was best able to fight. They believed in war, because they believed that just as nature removes the weak animal or plant by an early death, so the weak nation should pay the penalty of its weakness by being defeated in war and absorbed by the stronger one. War would prove which nation was the most nearly perfect. The Germans had no doubt that this nation was Germany. Acceptance of this belief by the German people had much to do with bringing on the present war.

Germany Wanted to Germanize the World. — As a result of the reasoning outlined in the last paragraph, German writers taught that those things which were German — their speech, their literature, their religion, their armies, in short the manners, customs, and thoughts of the Germans — were the best possible manners, and customs, and thoughts. These things all taken together are what is meant by *Kultur* (kool-toor′), — not merely "culture" as the latter word is generally used.

Since the Germans believed that their *Kultur* was the highest stage of human progress, the next step, according to the view of their leaders, would be to Germanize all the rest of the nations of the earth by imposing German *Kultur* upon them. If possible, this was to be brought about with the consent of the other nations; if not, then it was to be imposed by force.

Suggestions for Study. — 1. Locate Antwerp, Rotterdam, Hamburg, Bremen, East Prussia, Alsace-Lorraine. 2. Show on an outline map the regions which Germany desired to control. Who would have suffered? 3. If all countries adopted the German idea of war what would be the condition of the world? 4. Has any nation the right to impose its rule upon another people because it believes its own ideals are the only true ones?

References. — See page 26; also *Conquest and Kultur* (C. P. I.); *War Cyclopedia* (C. P. I.), under the headings "German Military Autocracy" and "Pan-Germanism."

CHAPTER III

GERMAN MILITARISM

What is Militarism? — Militarism has been defined as "a policy which maintains huge standing armies for purposes of aggression." It should be noticed that the mere fact that a nation, through universal conscription, maintains a large standing army in times of peace does not convict it of militarism. Every one of the great European powers except England maintained such an army, and yet Germany was the only one that we can say had a militaristic government.

A more narrow definition of militarism is that form of government in which the military power is in control, and with the slightest excuse can and does override the civil authority. This had been the situation in Germany for many years before the outbreak of the Great War.

Let us take a glance at the development of this sort of government. After Napoleon conquered Prussia, early in the nineteenth century, one of the conditions of peace was that Prussia should reduce her army to not more than forty-two thousand men. In order that the country should not again be so easily conquered, the king of Prussia enrolled the permitted number of men for one year, then dismissed that group, and enrolled another of the same size, and so on. Thus, in the course of ten years, it would be possible for him to gather an army of four hundred thousand men who had had at least one year of military training.

The officers of the army were drawn almost entirely from among the land-owning nobility. The result was that there was gradually built up a large class of military officers on the one hand, and, on the other, a much larger class, the rank and file of the army. These men had become used, in the army, to obeying implicitly all the commands of the officers.

This led to several results. Since the officer class furnished also most of the officials for the civil administration of the country, the interests of the army came to be considered the same as the interests of the country as a whole. A second result was that the governing class desired to continue a system which gave them so much power over the common people. We should perhaps consider as a third result the fact that the possession of such a splendid and efficient military machine tended to make its possessors arrogant and unyielding in their intercourse with other nations.

Competition in Armaments. — After 1870 the German emperor was the commander of the whole German army, which was organized and trained on the Prussian model. The fact that Germany had such an efficient army caused other nations to be in constant fear of attack. Therefore her neighbors on the continent of Europe were led to organize similar armies and make other preparations for defense.

Moreover, Germany in recent years formed a number of ambitious projects of expansion and colonization which would probably bring her into conflict with other countries. In order to assure herself of success, Germany proceeded to enlarge and otherwise improve the organization and equipment of her army. This led France and Russia to enlarge their armies. So the competition went on.

Germany's Navy.—For over a century Great Britain's control of the seas had been almost undisputed. In order to carry out her projects of expansion, Germany required a fleet which, while perhaps not so large as that of Great Britain, would be large enough to make the result of a naval battle questionable. Huge money grants were obtained from the German people, and for a time more battleships were built by Germany than by England. England dared not permit the naval superiority to pass into Germany's hands. The result was a competition in dreadnaught building quite as feverish as the competition in armies. The building and maintenance of these great fleets were a heavy burden upon the people of both countries. England made several offers to limit the competition by promising to build no ships in any year in which Germany would build none, but Germany in every case refused to agree to the plan.

Suggestions for Study. — 1. Make a chart showing the comparative sizes of European armies in 1914. 2. In the same way compare the European navies in 1914. 3. What effect is produced upon a country by an aristocratic military class? 4. Compare the German military policy with that of the United States. 5. Will disarmament be one of the good results of this war?

References. — The *World Almanac; War Cyclopedia* (C. P. I.), under the names of the several countries, and under "Navy"; *German Militarism* (C. P. I.).

CHAPTER IV

INTERNATIONAL LAW AND THE HAGUE CONFERENCES

International Law. — In the civilized world to-day each community is made up of citizens who have a right to the protection of the laws of their community and who in turn have the duty of obedience to those laws. During recent centuries improved means of communication and transportation have brought all parts of the world closer together, and there has grown up in the minds of many enlightened thinkers the idea that the whole civilized world ought to be regarded as a community of nations. In the past the relations of nations to one another have been very nearly as bad as that of persons in savage communities. Quarrels have usually been settled by contests of strength, called wars. Believers in the idea of the community of nations argue that wars would cease or at least become much less frequent if this idea of a community of nations were generally accepted.

The body of rules which nations recognize in their dealings with each other is usually spoken of as *international law.* As to certain rules of international conduct the civilized nations of the world have been in general agreement for many centuries. Among such rules are those for the carrying out of treaty obligations, the punishment of piracy, the protection of each other's ambassadors, the rights of citizens of one country to the protection of the laws of the country they are visiting, the protection of women and children in time of war.

As in community law so also in international law rules have frequently grown up as matters of custom. In the second place agreements have sometimes been reached through negotiation and written out in the form of treaties between the two nations concerned. In the latter half of the nineteenth century several attempts were made to strengthen international law by means of general conferences of the nations. One of the most famous of these was the Conference of Geneva in 1864, which reached a number of valuable agreements on the care of wounded soldiers and gave official international recognition to the Red Cross. At the very end of the century occurred the first of the two famous international conferences at The Hague.

Toward this growing movement in the direction of the setting up of a community of nations in which each has equal rights and equally recognizes the force of international law, the German Empire has taken an attitude of opposition. She has steadily refused to accept her place as a member of a family of nations. Her leaders have taken the ground, as explained in Chapter II, that strong nations should control weaker nations whenever it is to their own interest. As a principle this is just as barbarous as if in a community the man with the strongest muscles or the biggest club should be permitted to control the actions of his neighbors who happened to be weaker or less effectively armed. Just as the strong brutal man must be taught that laws apply to him as well as to the weaker members of the community, so must Germany learn to respect the laws of nations and the rights of weaker peoples.

The Call for a World Peace Conference. — In spite of the rapid growth of armaments in Europe after 1870 there was growing up among many of the leading thinkers of the nations a movement looking toward permanent peace in the world. The movement soon gained great strength among all classes. Peace societies were formed, meetings were held, and pamphlets were prepared and distributed. Toward the close of the century public opinion in most countries was leaning more and more toward the idea of universal peace. Governments, however, were slower to take up the problem. Strangely enough the first government to take action in the matter was that of Russia, at the time the most autocratic of all the nations of Europe.

Two years before the close of the century Czar Nicholas II sent out an official invitation calling upon the nations to send representatives to an international conference to discuss the problem of the prevention of wars. The Czar pointed out the dangers which must surely result if the military rivalry of the nations were not checked. He referred to the fact that European militarism was using up the strength and the wealth of the nations and was bringing about a condition of military preparedness which must inevitably lead in the end to a war more disastrous and terrible than any war in the history of mankind. The Czar did not go so far as to suggest complete and immediate disarmament. Every one knew that Europe was not ready to consider so violent a change of policy. The Russian invitation merely proposed that the conference should try to agree upon some means for putting a limit upon the increase of armaments. It suggested that the nations should agree not to increase their military or naval forces for a certain limited period, not to add to their annual expenditure of money for military purposes, and to consider means by which later on there might be an actual reduction of armaments. It was necessary to avoid the jealousies which might arise among the great powers if the capital of one of them were selected for the conference, so the Czar suggested that the meeting take place at The Hague, the capital of small, peace-loving Holland.

The First Hague Conference. — The conference called by the Czar met on May 18, 1899. All the great nations of the world sent delegates, as did many of the smaller nations. In all, twenty-six governments were represented, twenty of which were European. The United States and Mexico were the only countries of the New World which sent representatives. The queen of Holland showed her appreciation of the honor conferred upon her country by placing at the disposal of the conference, as its meeting place, the former summer residence of the royal family, the "House in the Woods," situated about a mile from the city in the midst of a beautiful park.

Disarmament. — Although the menace of the tremendous armaments of Europe had been the chief reason for the conference, absolutely nothing was accomplished toward solving that problem. This failure was largely due to the opposition of Germany, which, as the strongest military power in Europe, would listen to no suggestion looking toward the limitation of military force. At one of the early meetings of the conference a German delegate brought out clearly and unmistakably his government's opposition to any consideration of the subject. In a sarcastic and arrogant speech he defended the German system of compulsory military service and her expenditures for military purposes. While it is extremely doubtful, in view of the difficulties in the way of any general policy of disarmament, that much could have been accomplished by the conference even under the most favorable circumstances, this stand on the part of the German government meant the immediate and absolute defeat of the suggestion. The other nations of Europe had established their large military systems as a measure of defense against Germany, so that in the face of that government's refusal to agree to the policy of limiting armaments, no neighboring country on the European continent could adopt it. In the conference, the matter was dismissed after the adoption of a very general resolution expressing the opinion "that the restriction of military charges . . . is extremely desirable for the increase of the material and moral welfare of mankind."

Arbitration. — The conference met with a somewhat larger measure of success when it came to discuss the question of the peaceful settlement of international disputes, though here also the attitude of the German government stood in the way of complete success. The United States from the days of John Jay had taken the lead among the nations of the world in the policy of settling international disputes by peaceful means. Quite different has been the traditional policy of Prussia, which throughout its history has relied upon force to accomplish its purposes. All the German wars of the nineteenth century could easily have been averted if the Prussian government had honestly desired to settle its quarrels by peaceful methods. She has taken the ground, however, that arbitration can only work to her injury, since she is better prepared for war than any other nation and can mobilize her army more rapidly than any of her neighbors. "Arbitration," said one of her delegates at The Hague, "would simply give rival powers time to put themselves in readiness, and would therefore be a great disadvantage to Germany." This point of view shows clearly how the German leaders place the growth of German power far above such considerations as right and justice.

The Hague Peace Tribunal. — The struggle in the conference over the question of arbitration centered about the establishment of a permanent tribunal or international court of arbitration to which nations might bring their disagreements for settlement. The United States delegation favored making a definite list of the kinds of disputes which nations would be compelled to bring to the tribunal for settlement. On the other hand, the Kaiser himself sent a dispatch from Berlin in which he spoke strongly against anything in the nature of an arbitration tribunal. Largely through the efforts of Mr. Andrew D. White, head of the American delegation, the German government was brought to modify its stand. Germany finally agreed to the creation of the tribunal, but only on condition that in no case should the submission of a dispute to it be compulsory. The tribunal was to be established, but it would have the right to render a decision only in those cases which the disagreeing nations might decide to submit to it.

The Hague Tribunal is not made up of permanent judges like an ordinary court. It consists of persons (not more than four from each country) selected by the various nations from among their citizens of high standing and broad knowledge of international affairs. From this long list any powers between whom there is a disagreement may choose the persons to form a court or tribunal for their special case.

The Second Hague Conference. — The conference of 1899 had proved an absolute failure so far as disarmament and compulsory arbitration were concerned. In fact the years immediately following were marked by two destructive wars: that between Great Britain and the Boers of South Africa, and the war between Russia and Japan. These wars made it clear that with the applications of modern science warfare had become so terrible that, if the nations could not arrange by agreement for its abolition, they should at least take steps to lessen its horrors. This was the chief reason back of the invitation for a second Hague Conference, which was issued by the Czar at the suggestion of President Roosevelt. Forty-seven nations—nearly all the nations of the world—were represented when the conference assembled on June 15, 1907.

Attempts were made to reopen the questions of disarmament and compulsory arbitration, but without success. Germany again stood firmly against both suggestions. The conference consequently confined its efforts almost entirely to drawing up a code of international laws—especially those regulating the actual conduct of war—known as "the Hague Conventions." They contain rules about the laying of submarine mines, the treatment of prisoners, the bombardment of towns, and the rights of neutrals in time of war; they forbid, for example, the use of poison or of weapons causing unnecessary suffering. Even on these questions Germany stood out against certain changes which would have made war still more humane. But her delegates took part in framing the Hague Conventions; and Germany, like all the other powers later engaged in the Great

War, accepted those conventions by formal treaty, thus binding herself to observe them.

Results of the Hague Conferences.—Leaders of the movement for universal peace felt that in spite of the small success of the Hague Conferences a definite beginning had been made. Many of them were very hopeful that later conferences would lead to larger results and that even Germany would swing into line. There were plans to hold a third conference in 1914 or 1915. As we look back upon the years between 1907 and 1914, it seems hard to understand the general blindness of the world to the certainty of the coming struggle. Armaments were piled up at a faster rate than ever. Naval armaments also entered into the race. From the point of view of bringing about permanent peace in the world we must view the conferences at The Hague as having hopelessly failed.

They did accomplish something, however. Arbitration was accepted by the nations of the world, in principle at least. Moreover, the conferences helped the cause of international law by showing how easily international agreements could be reached if all the nations were honestly in favor of peaceful decisions. Some day when the present war has taught the world the much needed lessons that the recognition of international law is necessary to civilization, and that the nations must join together in its enforcement, the work begun at The Hague in 1899 and 1907 will be taken up once more with larger hope of success.

Suggestions for Study. — 1. How are ordinary laws enforced? How is international law carried out? Why the difference? 2. Enumerate the instances in which questions of international law have been brought up during the present war. 3. Look up the history of the Red Cross movement. 4. Why did the Hague Conferences fail to attain their great objects? 5. Summarize what was actually accomplished by the Conferences. 6. Has the history of the Hague Conferences any lessons which will be of value after this war?

References. — *War Cyclopedia* (C. P. I.), under "Red Cross," "Hague Conferences." See also publications of the World Peace Foundation; *International Conciliation* (C. P. I.); *War, Labor, and Peace* (C. P. I.).

CHAPTER V

INTERNATIONAL JEALOUSIES AND ALLIANCES

THE years between 1870 and 1914 were marked by growing jealousies among the great powers of Europe. All were growing in wealth and commerce, and each looked with envious eyes upon the successes of its neighbors. In this chapter we are going to consider some of the special reasons for the growth of international jealousies during this period, and the grouping of the great nations into alliances.

Alsace-Lorraine. — At the close of the Franco-Prussian War in 1871, France was humiliated by being forced to give up to Germany a large section of her eastern lands — Alsace and northeastern Lorraine. It was true that these provinces had long ago belonged to Germany. All of this territory, however, had been French for generations, and much of it for over two hundred years; and in both provinces the population was loyal to the French government and violently opposed to being transferred to the rule of Germany. But defeated France had no choice in the matter, and the provinces became part of the German Empire. France has never forgotten or forgiven this humiliation. Lloyd George, the British prime minister, in speaking of the Alsace-Lorraine problem (January, 1918) said, "This sore has poisoned the peace of Europe for half a century, and until it is cured healthy conditions cannot be restored."

German rule in Alsace-Lorraine has been unwise as well as severe. The teaching of the French language in the elementary schools of the provinces was forbidden. Military service in the German army was made compulsory despite the protests of the inhabitants, who felt a horror of some day being forced to fight against the French, whom they regarded as brothers.

All important offices were filled by Germans from beyond the Rhine. The police constantly interfered with the freedom of the people. French newspapers were suppressed on the slightest excuse. Attempts were made to prevent Frenchmen from visiting Alsace and Alsatians from visiting France. German army officers stationed in the provinces openly ignored the rights of the population and were upheld in their conduct by the German government. As time passed the inhabitants grew more and more dissatisfied with the strict German rule.

In France also hostility to Germany was increased by the conditions in Alsace-Lorraine. Frenchmen could not forget that they had been robbed of these provinces. Hope was kept alive that some day they might be won back. In the city of Paris, in the Place de la Concorde, there are eight large marble statues each representing a great city of France. One of these represents Strassburg, the chief city of Alsace. Every year, on July 14, the national holiday of France, the people of Paris have placed a wreath of mourning on this statue. This custom expresses the sorrow of France for the loss of her eastern provinces, as well as her hope that some day they may be restored.

Italia Irredenta. — *Italia Irreden'ta* in the Italian language means "unredeemed Italy." It refers to the territory adjoining Italy on the north and northeast, occupied by Italians but not yet redeemed from foreign rule.

When in 1871 the kingdom of Italy took its present form through the union of former Italian states (Chapter I), Italia Irredenta remained under the rule of Austria.

Italians feel, however, that Italian unity is not complete so long as adjoining lands inhabited by Italian-speaking people are ruled by foreign governments. So they regard these lands as "unredeemed."

Italia Irredenta consists chiefly of the Trentino (tren-tee′no), a triangle of territory dipping down into the north of Italy, and some land around the northern end of the Adriatic including the important city of Trieste. Both of these regions are ruled by Austria. For many years this situation has led to ill feeling between the two countries. While it has not had so direct a bearing on the outbreak of the World War as the question of Alsace-Lorraine, it nevertheless largely explains the entrance of Italy into the war on the side of the Allies.

Russia and the Bosporus. — Still another situation which in the years before the war was the cause of international jealousies was Russia's long-standing ambition to control Constantinople on the Bos′porus. As Constantinople is the capital of the Turkish Empire, the continued existence of that state, at least on the continent of Europe, was threatened by Russia's purpose. Russia has long been in need of an ice-free port as an outlet for her commerce. Archangel (ark′ān′jel) in the north is ice-bound most of the year. Vladivostok′, her port on the Pacific, is ice-bound for three months of the year. Russian trade by way of the Baltic must pass through waters controlled by other countries. Naturally she has turned toward the Bosporus and Dardanelles (dar-da-nelz′) — the straits connecting the Black Sea with the Mediterranean — as the natural outlet for her trade, and this explains her desire to possess Constantinople.

For centuries Russia has been so much more powerful than Turkey that she would surely have taken possession of Constantinople if the other nations of Europe had not interfered. On two different occasions during the nineteenth century England came to the assistance of the Turkish Empire and saved Constantinople from the Czar. Great Britain was led to take this action through fear that Russian control of Constantinople might endanger the safety of her own communications with India. In the years immediately preceding the outbreak of the Great War the danger from Germany made other quarrels of much less importance, and England's disagreement with Russia over her desire for a trade outlet was forgotten.

European Ambitions in the Balkans. — Russia has always felt a strong interest in the small nations of the Balkan peninsula. Their inhabitants are for the most part Slavs, of the same race as the Russians themselves, and they have naturally looked upon the great Slavic empire of the Czars as their protector. There was, moreover, a pan-Slavic party in Russia, i.e. a group who looked forward to a union of all the Slav nations under the leadership of Russia. The pan-Slavic movement had its beginning in the help Russia had given these states in their revolt from Turkey.

Russia's aims and hopes in the Balkans were strongly opposed by Austria-Hungary. That state has long felt the need of seaports to the southeast and has hoped, with German support, to secure an outlet on the Ægean and to control the whole course of the Danube. This purpose could be accomplished only by annexing a large part of the Balkan peninsula. The Balkan situation, therefore, brought Russia and Austria face to face in opposition to each other. It was one of the most serious instances of international rivalry in the period before the war.

Italy also was interested in the Balkan question. She saw that if the Austrians should annex the Balkan lands lying to the south they would control the whole eastern shore of the Adriatic. Italian interests and ambitions would suffer. This fear, added to the constant bitterness caused by the problem of Italia Irredenta, inflamed the hostility of Italy toward Austria.

Finally, Turkey also had an interest in the Balkan situation. She hoped to benefit by the various jealousies of the great powers. She believed that fear of a general war would keep all of them from making any move in the Balkans and so would prolong her own shaky existence as a European state.

Rival Colonial Empires. — Some time after the establishment of the German Empire, her rapidly growing wealth, population, and trade led her to regret the opportunities for colonial expansion that she had missed. She cast jealous eyes upon the vast colonial possessions of other nations. She also took what was left over, — several large regions of Africa, a port in China, a few islands in the Pacific, — not nearly enough to satisfy her ambitions. South America was closed to her by the policy of the United States which is expressed in the Monroe Doctrine. In Asia, however, she secured extensive commercial and industrial concessions — the forerunners of political control — in the Turkish Empire. Germany's desire for colonies was natural enough, but her jealousy of her more fortunate European neighbors must be considered as one of the reasons underlying her military and naval preparedness for war.

Germany's covetous attitude toward the colonial possessions of other nations led to several serious international disagreements in the years before the Great War. More than once it almost brought her into conflict with the government of the United States. An agreement had been made for the joint control of the Samoan Islands by Great Britain, Germany, and the United States. Germany's attempt to enlarge her interests in the islands led to a quarrel with American officers. An American flag was seized by armed Germans, war vessels were sent to Samoa, and a naval battle seemed about to take place. A hurricane destroyed the vessels, however, before any fighting had occurred, and the three countries drew up a treaty which settled that particular difficulty (1899).

Germany also resented our acquisition of the Philippines and other Spanish colonies. At the outbreak of our war with Spain in 1898, when Admiral Dewey steamed into Manila Bay, he found there a German fleet that was half disposed to interfere with his operations. But when Dewey showed a willingness to fight, the Germans withdrew.

Several years later Germany picked a quarrel with Venezuela and, in defiance of the Monroe Doctrine, bombarded a fort on her coast. Acting in conjunction with England and Italy, German warships blockaded the ports of Venezuela to force the payment of financial claims. President Roosevelt's insistence that Germany drop her further plans of aggression, and his promptness in concentrating the American fleet in the West Indies, resulted in Germany's accepting a peaceful solution of the dispute.

In 1911 Germany tried to force France out of Morocco. Since 1904 France had by common consent taken general charge of affairs in that country. Later Germany made objections to this arrangement. Finally, in 1911, when France was sending troops into the interior to put down disorders among the natives, Germany sent a gunboat to Agadir (ah-gah-deer'), on the west coast of Morocco. It looked as if she intended to take possession of the port there. France protested and the affair began to look very warlike. England came to the support of France, and Germany gave up all claim to Morocco, taking in exchange about 100,000 square miles in equatorial Africa. After this humiliation the German militarists became more determined than ever to force the war which they thought would make Germany supreme over her rivals.

The Triple Alliance. — The various jealousies among the nations of Europe which we have just considered, and particularly the general fear of the growing power of the German Empire, largely explain the strong international alliances which came into existence between 1870 and 1914.

Germany, after 1870, knew that France would for many years be too weak to retake Alsace-Lorraine. All that German leaders had to fear was that France might succeed in securing powerful friends among the other nations and that a strong combination of countries might some day challenge Germany's supremacy on the Continent. To prevent or at any rate to counterbalance any such combination, Germany looked about for allies upon whose help she might rely in case of necessity. At first she planned a general league of friendship with the great countries lying to the east and southeast, Russia and Austria-Hungary. This combination, known as the League of the Three Emperors, was soon broken up by the growing jealousies of Russia and Austria in the Balkans. Germany, having to choose which of these two nations she would support, decided in favor of Austria. There followed a growing coldness in the relations between Germany and Russia.

Germany having allied herself with Austria, looked about for another nation to give greater strength to the combination. Her thoughts turned toward Italy, which, in case of another war against France, could attack the French southeastern border and so prove a valuable ally. For a number of years there had been ill feeling between Italy and France, and Germany counted on this feeling to bring Italy under her influence. The chief difficulty in the way of Germany's plan was that Italy would have to abandon her ideas in regard to Italia Irredenta and enter into friendly relations with Austria, her old enemy. Italy was finally driven into this unnatural alliance by the action of France, which in 1881 occupied Tunis, a land which Italy herself had been planning to annex as a colony. Italy, too weak to prevent this action of France, entered the alliance with Germany and Austria into which she had been invited. So it was that the Triple Alliance was established (1882), as a league of defense against any nations which should begin an attack upon any one of the three.

The Triple Entente. — *Entente* (ahn-tahnt') is the French word for understanding or agreement. In the recent history of Europe it refers to that friendly grouping of nations which was formed in self-defense against the Triple Alliance. The war of 1870 had left France not only humiliated but weakened and isolated. The formation of the Triple Alliance put out of question the idea of a successful war against Germany to right the wrong which France had suffered. In fact it seemed to make more probable a new attack upon France. Russia also found herself in a position of isolation. Their isolation and consequent danger gradually drew these two nations together, distant as they were from one another and different as they were in government and ideas. So there was established a dual alliance between the French Republic and the Russian Empire.

Great Britain had for a long time remained outside the jealousies and combinations of the continental powers. In fact she had frequently found herself at odds with France over the rights of the two nations in Africa, and with Russia over the question of Constantinople and Russian aggression in Asia. When English statesmen discovered, however, that the German Empire was constantly enlarging her navy with a view to challenging English control of the seas, they felt that it would be well for Great Britain to seek friendships on the Continent. Old quarrels with France and Russia were forgotten. Friendly relations were established, and Great Britain, France, and Russia entered into a league of friendship known as the Triple Entente (1907).

Suggestions for Study. — 1. Locate the Bosporus, Alsace-Lorraine, Italia Irredenta, Balkan peninsula, Ægean Sea. 2. Explain the geographical importance of Constantinople. How was Russia prevented from taking it in the Crimean War of 1854 and the Russo-Turkish War of 1877? 3. Show on a map of Europe the countries in the Triple Alliance and those in the Triple Entente. Why was each alliance formed?

References. — *War Cyclopedia* (C. P. I.); Harding, *New Medieval and Modern History;* Hazen, *Europe since* 1815; and other European histories. For the treaties forming the two alliances, see *A League of Nations*, Vol. I, No. 4.

CHAPTER VI

THE BALKAN STATES

The Balkans. — As we have learned in Chapter I, the Balkan states are, with the exception of Montenegro, the result of a series of revolutions which took place during the last hundred years. These revolutions were the result of two causes. First there was a growing restlessness of the different groups of people in the Balkan peninsula. This was due not only to centuries of Turkish misrule, but also to the influence of the republican movement which developed in northern and western Europe as a result of the French Revolution. The second cause of the Balkan revolutions was the gradual growth among the oppressed races of the feeling that they would better their condition by throwing off the despotic Turkish rule and by organizing each separate race into a separate nation. Thus it was that the revolutions brought into existence a group of small states, each populated chiefly by one of the races inhabiting the Balkans.

Races in the Balkans. — There are more races represented in the Balkans than in any similar sized territory in Europe. Most of the Balkan states lie along what was the northeastern fringe of the Roman Empire. So we find inhabiting them not only ancient races like the Greeks and Albanians, but also descendants of

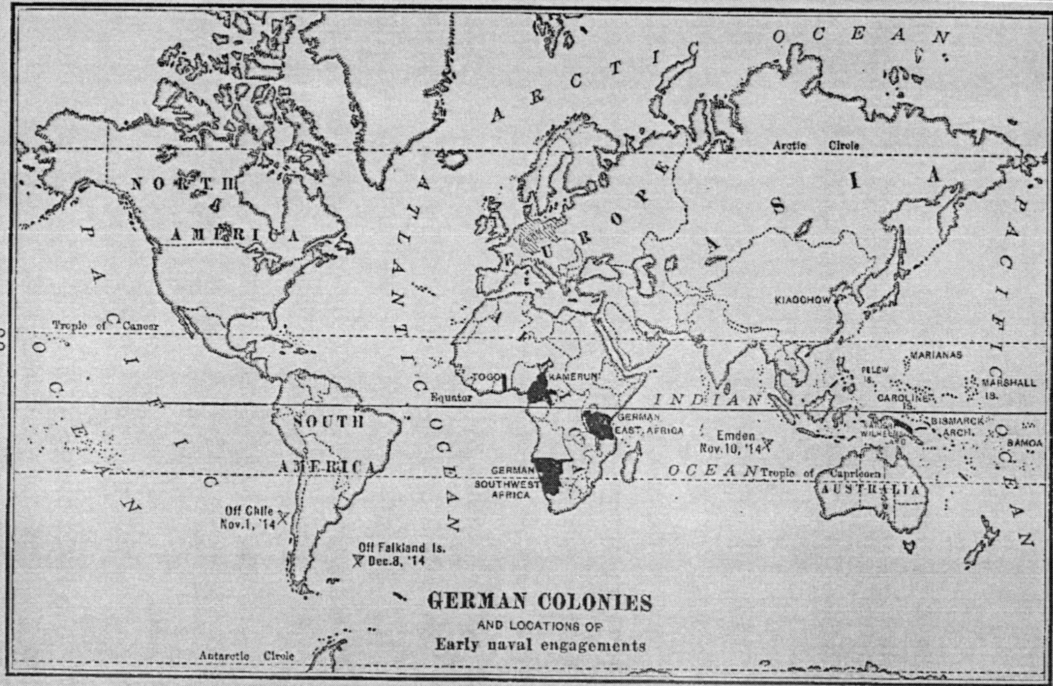

GERMAN COLONIES
AND LOCATIONS OF
Early naval engagements

Roman colonists like the Roumanians, and other racial groups like the Serbs and Bulgars, which represent the survivals of the barbarian invasions of the Middle Ages. While the larger groups of invaders passed on to the west, these dropped out and moved southward into the Balkan peninsula, where their descendants still remain. We must not think that these are pure races. There has been much intermixture, and to-day all of the groups contain a strong Slavic element, although some are rather unwilling to admit it. There is besides a Turkish element in the population, as the result of the long period of Turkish rule, especially in those districts where many of the original inhabitants accepted Mohammedanism, as in Albania and Macedonia.

The Slavs. — The Serbs, a Slavic race, form the chief part of the population in Serbia and Montenegro, as well as in Bosnia and other parts of southern Austria-Hungary. Together with the Croats and Slovenes of southern Austria-Hungary, the Serbs are called the Jugo-Slavs (yoo′go-slavz) or South-Slavs (*jugo* means "south") to distinguish them from the Czechs, Poles, and Russians of the north. There is, however, a strong feeling of relationship between these two great Slavic groups.

The Bulgars. — The Bulgars are descended from a non-Slavic race allied to the Tatars and Finns. They came into the Balkan region on the heels of some of the early migrations and seized the land now called Bulgaria; there, however, they mingled with the native Slavic people whom they conquered, and whose language they adopted. There are, besides, many Bulgarians in the Dobrud'ja — the district lying between the lower Danube and the Black Sea. Likewise in the province of Macedonia, the Bulgarians form the largest element in the population.

The Roumanians. — Roumania is the old Roman province of Dacia, and the Roumanians claim to be descendants of colonists which the Romans sent into that province as an outpost against invasion. It is certain that the language spoken by the Roumanians is much like Latin, but, as a recent writer says, the language is closer to Latin than the Roumanians are to Romans.

The Albanians. — The Albanian people are descended from the most ancient of all the races in the Balkan peninsula; their language is the oldest language spoken in Europe. For centuries they were nominally subject to Turkey; but the Turks never really succeeded in conquering them, though many of the Albanians became Mohammedans.

The Greeks. — Though the Greeks are descended in part from the people who inhabited their country in ancient times, and though they speak a modern form of the old Greek language, it is certain that the present inhabitants are a much mixed race. They are largely Slav, but hold a strong feeling for the great past of their country. This gives them an unusually strong national rallying point. In many ways the Greeks are the most progressive of the Balkan races.

Russia and Austria as Protectors of the Balkan Countries. — The struggle between the great powers as to which of them should become the heirs of "the sick man of Europe," as the Sultan of Turkey was long ago called, dates back about a century. Austria on account of her geographical position and her desire to expand to the southward, and Russia on account of her desire for Constantinople and the racial ties connecting her with the Balkan states, each hoped to be preferred. Both Austria and Russia, then, for more or less selfish reasons, were anxious to bring about the break-up of the Turkish Empire in Europe. Whenever a revolt against Turkish rule would break out, the revolutionists could almost always count on the help of one or the other of these nations.

Since the Slavs and the Greeks hated each other, and both hated the Bulgarians, there was sometimes a tendency for the Bulgarians and the Greeks to look to Austria or Germany for help, as a counterpoise to Russia's influence on behalf of the Slavic states. At one time, however, Russia gave great aid to Bulgaria. In all the twists and turns of Balkan politics we find Russia or Austria posing as protector of the rights of one or another of the Balkan states.

On the other hand, when all the Balkan states bordering Turkey put aside their rivalries and combined for an attack on Turkey in 1912, Germany and Austria gave what moral support they could to Turkey. Austria had no desire to see a strong league of the Balkan states formed to the south of her, a league which would be largely under the influence of Russia.

German leaders had already formulated their dream of *Mittel-Europa* (Mid-Europe), a broad band of German-controlled territory extending to Turkey. With Turkey itself Germany made treaties which practically assured her control all the way to Bagdad. Germany had no desire either for a Balkan league, which would block her way, or for the defeat of Turkey, which might interfere with the carrying out of the treaties.

The Balkan War of 1912. — Turkish rule in Macedonia had become increasingly bad. Situated in the midst of three of the larger Balkan countries, it had representatives of each among its population. These countries put aside for the time being their jealousies of each other. In 1912 Bulgaria, Greece, Serbia, and Montenegro formed an alliance and presented a demand to Turkey that Macedonia should be made self-governing. Most of Europe believed that the German-trained army of the Turks would annihilate the armies of the smaller nations. But in a little over a month Turkey was beaten. Even Constantinople might have been taken had Bulgaria pursued the advantage gained by her troops. This time no nation protected Turkey, and the treaty of peace left her with only a tiny bit of European territory and the city of Constantinople. Incidentally, Germany had lost much prestige, for Turkey had fought the war with the help of German officers and with German encouragement, and had lost.

The Second Balkan War. — Unfortunately, the victors soon quarreled over the spoils. Bulgaria had seized Thrace and wanted most of Macedonia, including the city of Saloni′ca, which had been captured by the Greeks. Austria intervened to prevent Serbia from getting any increase in territory on the southwest, toward the Adriatic. Hence Serbia wanted a share of the lands to the south, claimed by Bulgaria. Bulgaria, backed by Austria and Germany, refused to make any concessions, or to leave the dispute to arbitration. She began the second Balkan war with a night attack on the Serbian and Greek armies, but was unable to defeat them. On the contrary Bulgaria was defeated within a month, partly because Roumania and Turkey also entered the struggle against her. Bulgaria had to give up much of her conquests to her former allies. Roumania claimed a slice off her northeastern corner, and a Turkish army recaptured Adrianople and neighboring territory from the hard-pressed Bulgarians.

Loss of Prestige by Germany and Austria. — One of the important results of these two wars was the loss of prestige by Germany and Austria. These "Central Powers," as they were called, had gone out of their way to encourage first Turkey, and then Bulgaria, and both these countries had been badly beaten. In any future diplomacy the opinions and desires of the Central Powers would have less weight and impressiveness than formerly. To regain their lost influence it was practically certain that these nations would, at the earliest opportunity, make an attempt to impose their will upon the victorious Balkan states.

Suggestions for Study. — 1. Locate Macedonia, the Dobrudja, Nish, Sofia, Durazzo. 2. Define and explain Mittel-Europa; "The sick man of Europe." 3. Which nations of the Balkan peninsula border upon the Black Sea? Which border upon the Adriatic? Which lie along the Danube? 4. On an outline map of the Balkan peninsula indicate the races to which the populations belong and their distribution. 5. We have read in this chapter that the old Roman province of Dacia developed later into modern Roumania; can you name the Roman provinces which correspond to the modern nations of France, Spain, England, Switzerland? 6. What do you know of the history of Constantinople prior to its capture by the Turks? 7. Explain the causes of the second Balkan war. How did the outcome of this war affect the history of the great European powers?

References. — *War Cyclopedia* (C. P. I.); *Study of the Great War* (C. P. I.); Davis, *The Roots of the War;* Hazen, *Europe since 1815;* and other general histories of recent Europe.

CHAPTER VII

THE BEGINNINGS OF THE GREAT WAR

Germany's Responsibility. — Germany's tremendous increase of armaments, her opposition to arbitration, her hostility to the purpose of the Hague Conferences, her building up of the Triple Alliance, her challenge to England's naval supremacy and her refusal to accept England's suggestion that both nations should limit their expenditures on naval armaments, the glorification of war on the part of her teachers and writers, — all make it clear that the present Great War was of her planning. For years she prepared herself to inflict a crushing blow with all the weight of her powerful army and navy and establish herself as the mistress of the world. On this she was willing to stake her very existence. To use a phrase made famous by one of her leading military writers, Germany had decided upon "world power or downfall."

German militarists all looked forward to the day when her years of preparation would at last reap their reward through the crushing of Germany's rivals. England particularly, with her vast trade, her colonial empire, and her control of the sea, they planned to lower to a subordinate position in the world. "*Der Tag*" (dĕr tähkh), "the day" when the long-awaited war should burst upon the world, was a favorite toast in the German army and navy. As long ago as the end of the Spanish-American War, a German diplomat said to an American army officer: "About fifteen years from now my country will start her great war. She will be in Paris in about two months after the commencement of hostilities. Her move on Paris will be but a step to her real object — the crushing of England. Everything will move like clockwork. We will be prepared and others will not be prepared."

Final Preparations.—In 1913 the German government decided upon a large increase in her already tremendous standing army. Immense sums were also appropriated for aircraft and for huge guns powerful enough to batter to pieces the strongest fortresses. To pay for this extra equipment additional heavy taxes were voted. The new arrangements were all to be completed by the fall of 1914. Alterations were also hurried on the Kiel Canal. This waterway, connecting the Baltic with the North Sea, had been opened in 1895 and was of great naval importance. The new German battleships, however, were so large that the canal was not large enough to admit them. The work of widening and deepening the passage was undertaken by the government, and was finally completed on July 1, 1914. Preparations for the Great War were complete at last, both on land and sea. The gunpowder was ready. All that was needed was a spark to bring about the explosion.

The Austro-Serbian Question. — For years before the war the Serbs and other Jugo-Slavs in the southern provinces of Austria-Hungary had been dissatisfied with Austrian rule. The Serbs of Bosnia and Herzegovina (hĕr-tsĕ-go-vee′nah) were especially aroused when those provinces, after a long temporary government by Austria-Hungary, were formally annexed by that power in 1908. Their wish was for union with the adjoining Serbian kingdom. Their aspirations did not cause very much trouble while Serbia was small and weak; but when, as a result of the Balkan wars, Serbia was revealed to the world as a warlike nation with extended boundaries and growing national ambitions, the Austrian Serbs grew restless. There is little doubt that Serbs of Serbia had much to do with the anti-Austrian activities that rapidly spread among their brothers within the Austrian Empire. The Austrian government, much disturbed by a movement that threatened to spread among her other subject populations, began to seek a pretext for crushing her southern neighbor and so settling the troublesome Serbian question once for all.

In 1913, at the close of the second Balkan war, Austria-Hungary informed her allies, Italy and Germany, of her intention to make war upon Serbia, and asked for the support of those countries. Italy refused to have any part in the matter. Germany, realizing that Russia would probably come to the assistance of Serbia and that a general European war might follow, no doubt prevailed upon Austria to stay her hand. Germany's preparations at that time were not quite complete.

The Assassination of Francis Ferdinand. — In the early summer of 1914 occurred the event that was destined to plunge the world into war. Archduke Francis Ferdinand, heir to the throne of Austria-Hungary, made a visit to the southern provinces of the monarchy. On June 28, while he and his wife were driving through the streets of Serajevo (sĕr'a-yā-vo), in Bosnia, three pistol shots were fired into the carriage, mortally wounding the archduke and his wife. The assassin was an Austrian Serb, a member of a Serbian secret society which had for its aim the separation of the Serb provinces from Austria-Hungary and their annexation to the kingdom of Serbia. The crime caused great excitement and horror throughout Europe. But the deed had given Austria the opportunity to settle its account with Serbia and thus put an end to the Serb plottings within the Austrian borders.

The Decision for War. — There is evidence that on July 5, one week after the murder at Serajevo, a secret meeting of German and Austrian statesmen and generals took place in the German emperor's palace at Potsdam, a suburb of Berlin. Probably at this conference it was definitely decided that the assassination of the Austrian crown prince should be used as a pretext for crushing Serbia. Austria, it was expected, would thus permanently settle her Serbian problem. Germany must have known that this action would probably lead to a general European war, since Russia would come to the rescue of Serbia and France would stand by Russia.

But Germany was ready at last, and so the terrible decision was made.

The Austrian Ultimatum. — On July 23, the Austro-Hungarian government sent a note to the government of Serbia holding her accountable for the Serajevo murder and making a number of humiliating demands. Serbia was told she must suppress all newspapers inciting enmity to Austria, that she must dissolve all societies that were working toward "Pan-Serbism," that she must dismiss from the Serbian public service all officials whom the Austrian government should officially accuse of plotting against Austria, that she must accept the help of Austrian officials in Serbia in the putting down of anti-Austrian activities and in searching out accessories to the plot of June 28, that she must arrest two Serbian officials who had been implicated by the trial in Serajevo, and that she must put a stop to the smuggling of arms from Serbia into Austria.

The demand that Serbia admit Austrian officials into Serbia to take part in the work of investigation and suppression was an intolerable invasion of Serbia's sovereignty within her own borders. But the most threatening part of the note was its conclusion: "The Austro-Hungarian government expects the reply of the royal [Serbian] government at the latest by 6 o'clock on Saturday evening, the 25th of July." In other words, the note was an ultimatum giving Serbia a period of only forty-eight hours in which to agree to the Austrian demands.

Serbia's Reply. — Serbia's answer to the Austrian ultimatum was delivered within a few minutes of the time set. She agreed, practically, to all the Austrian demands except those which required that Austrian officials should conduct investigations and suppress conspiracies in Serbia, and she even went part way toward accepting those. Serbia went on to suggest that if Austria was not entirely satisfied with the reply, the points still in dispute should be referred to the international tribunal at The Hague. This reply the Austrian government considered unsatisfactory. Forty-five minutes after the Serbian note had been placed in the hands of the Austrian minister to Serbia that official handed a notice to the Serbian government stating "that not having received a satisfactory answer within the time limit set, he was leaving Belgrade" (the Serbian capital). Austria-Hungary made immediate preparations for the invasion of Serbia and on July 28 declared war.

Efforts for Peace. — Meanwhile Great Britain, France, and Italy were putting forth every effort to preserve the peace of Europe. In these efforts the lead was taken by Sir Edward Grey, the British foreign minister. As early as July 26 he urged a conference at London of the representatives of France, Germany, Italy, and Great Britain to find some solution of the problem which might be satisfactory to both Austria and Russia. Italy and France agreed at once, but Germany raised objections. Germany's only suggestion for preserving the general peace of Europe was that

Austria should be permitted to deal with Serbia as she pleased, without interference from any other power. And so it continued through those critical days. Every effort made by England looking toward a peaceful settlement of the quarrel was baffled by Germany's refusal to coöperate. This is not difficult to understand in the light of our later knowledge of the plans and aims of the German government.

The Declarations of War. — Austria's declaration of war on Serbia (July 28) was followed by the general mobilization of Austria's troops. Austria maintained that all her armies were for the war on Serbia, but her preparations were so extensive that it was clear she was getting ready to fight Russia also. In reply Russia began to mobilize her troops, partly to prevent the destruction of Serbia, but also to defend herself from possible Austrian attacks. Russia definitely notified Germany that her mobilization was directed against Austria only. Meanwhile England continued her efforts to bring about a conference of the powers, a plan which Germany continued to foil. The Czar in a formal telegram to the Kaiser on July 29 suggested that the Austro-Serbian problem be given over to the Hague Tribunal, a suggestion which would have led to peace. Nothing came of this proposal.

On July 31 the German government, on the ground that Russia's mobilization was a threat of war, sent ultimatums to both Russia and France. The ultimatum to Russia gave that government twelve hours in which to stop all war preparations against both Germany and Austria. The ultimatum to France informed that government of the message just sent to Russia, and demanded a reply within eighteen hours as to whether France would remain neutral in case of war between Germany and Russia. The crowds in the streets of Berlin went wild with joy over the news of the two ultimatums. There were cries of "On to Paris" and "On to St. Petersburg." The Kaiser addressed his people from the balcony of his palace. In the course of his speech, he said, "The sword is being forced into our hand." The government of Germany had decided to make its people believe that they were about to fight in self-defense.

Russia would not demobilize her armies under a German threat. Consequently the next day, August 1, Germany declared war upon Russia. Two days later, August 3, Germany declared war on France because that country had refused to desert her ally in this time of danger. The greatest war of all history had begun.

Great Britain Enters the War. — The German military leaders felt sure that Great Britain would remain neutral in case of a general European war. They based this belief on the peaceful temper of the English people, upon the serious domestic problems she was facing, such as the question of woman suffrage, Irish Home Rule, and the threatening labor situation. Germany regarded England as a nation of shopkeepers who would not fight unless they were attacked. After Germany had made herself supreme on the Continent England's turn would come.

Great Britain's agreement with France and Russia, the other members of the Triple Entente, did not go so far as to require her to join them in case they should be involved in war. It is difficult to say whether or not Great Britain would have decided to enter the conflict at this time if a new element had not been introduced into the question by Germany's invasion of Belgium. Of this invasion more will be said in the following chapter. All that need be mentioned here is that Germany, in spite of a long-standing treaty to observe Belgium's neutrality, had decided on marching through that country as the best route to Paris. Great Britain, as one of the nations which had promised to protect the neutrality of Belgium, immediately demanded of the German government that it withdraw its plan of invasion. Germany refused, and on August 4 Great Britain declared war. So one week after Austria's declaration of war against Serbia all the powers of the Triple Entente — commonly called the Allies — were in arms against Germany and Austria. Italy, the third member of the Triple Alliance, on August 1 declared herself neutral, much to the disappointment and anger of the Central Powers, her former allies. Her treaty with them provided that she should come to their aid only in case they were attacked, and so did not apply to the present war, in which Germany and Austria were the aggressors.

Suggestions for Study. — 1. Locate the Kiel Canal. What is its other name? When and why was it constructed? 2. Locate Potsdam, Belgrade, Serajevo. 3. Define ultimatum; mobilization; "Der Tag"; Jugo-Slavs. 4. What is the meaning of the prefix "pan" in Pan-Slavism, Pan-Germanism, Pan-Serbism? What do you know about each of these movements? 5. What is a declaration of war? Who has the power to declare war in the United States? In Germany? 6. Where are the provinces of Bosnia and Herzegovina? How were they governed before 1878? Between 1878 and 1908? Since 1908? 7. Review the efforts for peace made by the British government between the Austrian ultimatum and Germany's final declarations of war. Explain the attitude of Austria, Russia, France, and Germany during these days.

References. — *War Cyclopedia* (C. P. I.); *Study of the Great War* (C. P. I.); *The Government of Germany* (C. P. I.); Davis, *The Roots of the War*.

CHAPTER VIII

THE WAR IN 1914

German Plan of Attack.—As soon as the German leaders had determined upon war, their military machine was set in motion. The plan was first to attack France and crush her armies before the slow-moving Russians could get a force together; and then, after the defeat of France, to turn to the east and subdue Russia. The success of the plan was dependent upon the swift overthrow of France; and this in turn hinged upon the question as to whether German armies could invade France before the French were ready. Speed was the essential thing, and in order to gain speed Germany committed one of the greatest crimes in modern history.

From the nearest point on the German boundary to Paris is only one hundred and seventy miles. But no rapid invasion of France could be made in this direction for two reasons: first, because of the very strong forts which protected the French frontier; and second, on account of the nature of the land, which presents to the east a series of five easily defended ridges, each of which would have to be stormed by an invader. A German attack directly across the French frontier could move but slowly past these natural and military obstacles; and the French nation would have ample time to mobilize its forces.

Consequently the German military leaders determined to attack France from the northeast. Here a comparatively level plain stretched from Germany through Belgium and France up to Paris itself. Many good roads and railways traversed the land. Few natural barriers existed to aid the defenders, and France, trusting to the neutrality of Belgium, had no strong fortifications on her northeastern frontier. One obstacle to German invasion existed; it was what the German Chancellor once[1] called "a scrap of paper"—a promise to respect the neutrality of Belgium, which Prussia, France, and England had agreed to by formal treaties. Similar treaties guaranteed the neutrality of Luxemburg, a small country east of Belgium. Upon these promises France had depended for the protection of her northeastern border; for the German Empire had accepted all the rights and all the duties of the treaties made by Prussia. But now, under the plea of necessity which "knows no law," the German rulers determined to break their promises, violate the neutrality of Belgium and Luxemburg, and crush France before an aroused and alarmed world could interfere.

Belgium Blocks the German Plan.—The invasion of Belgium had two results which the Germans had not foreseen. In the first place, it brought Great

[1] In an interview with the British ambassador, as reported by the ambassador, August 4, 1914.

Britain immediately into the war to the aid of Belgium and France. In the second place, the Belgian king and people refused to be bought off with a promise of compensation; they made the high decision to defend their country as long as possible against the terrible German army-machine. Said the Belgian king: "A country which defends itself commands the respect of all; that country cannot perish." This action of Belgium disarranged the German army plans; instead of reaching Paris according to schedule, the Germans were delayed in Belgium for ten days. These ten days were full of horror and suffering and defeat for the brave Belgians; but they are precious days in the light of history. They gave time for the French to mobilize their armies and bring them up to the northeast; and they enabled Great Britain to send across the English Channel her first hundred thousand troops. In this way Paris was saved from capture, and France from conquest; and probably the whole world from German domination. The German plans for world conquest met their first defeat at the hands of brave little Belgium. The would-be conquerors had forgotten to include in their time-table the elements of honor, patriotism, and self-sacrifice.

The German Advance.—Luxemburg was occupied without resistance, for that little country had no army. On August 4, 1914, the German armies attacked the Belgian fortress of Liege (lee-ĕzh′), and within twenty-three days Belgium was overrun, its capital taken, and all the important places except Antwerp captured. After the delay in Belgium, the main German armies advanced into France. Here they were met (August 21–23) by French and British troops; but the defenders were not

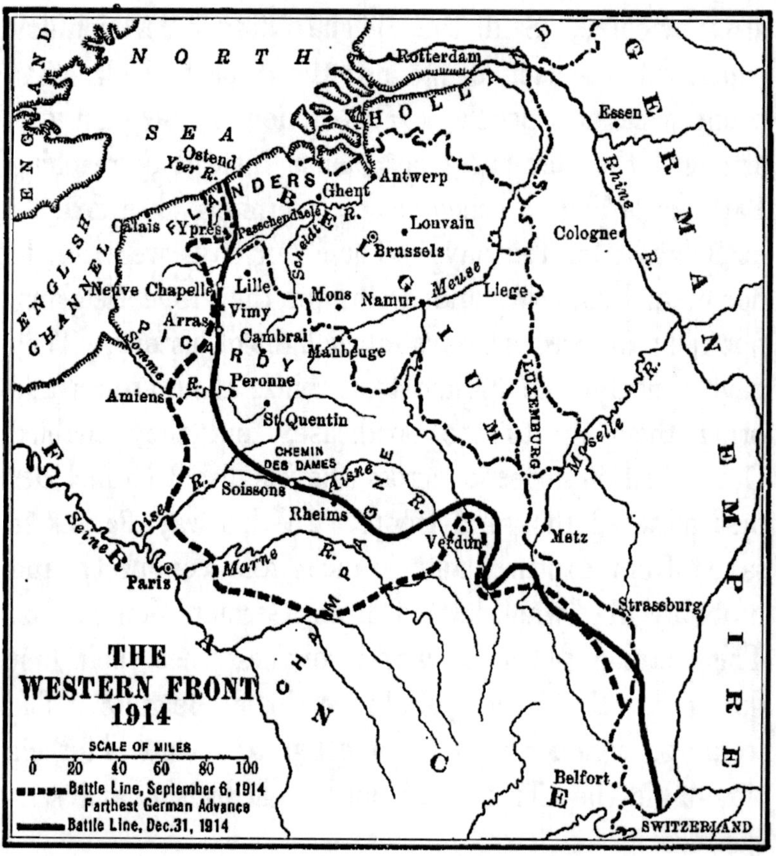

yet strong enough to stop the German advance. For twelve days they fell back toward Paris, fighting continually, until the invaders were within twenty miles of the city. The French government and archives were withdrawn from Paris to Bordeaux in the southwest, so imminent seemed the capture of the capital. The battle line now extended for one hundred and seventy-five miles eastward from near Paris to the fortress of Verdun.

The First Battle of the Marne.—In the meantime the French commander, General Joffre (zhofr), had secretly been collecting another army with which to attack the invaders on the flank from the west. At the right moment he hurled this army upon the German flank, while the men on the main battle line were commanded to "face about and accept death rather than surrender." On September 6–10 took place the first great battle of the Marne, during which the Germans, under these new attacks, were compelled to retreat fifty miles from their most advanced position. The French armies had rescued Paris in the nick of time. The French government once more returned to its capital. "France had saved herself and Europe."

The Race to the Coast.—On reaching the river Aisne (ân) the German armies had time to entrench themselves and thus beat off the heavy attacks of the French and British (September 12–17). The Allied armies in turn began to entrench opposite the German positions. But both armies turned toward the north in a race to reach the North Sea and outflank the enemy. The Germans were particularly anxious to reach Calais (ca-lĕ′) and cut the direct line of communication between England and France. Antwerp surrendered to the Germans on October 9; Lille (leel) on the 13th.

In tremendous massed attacks the Germans sought in vain to break through the British lines (Battle of Flanders, October 17 to November 15). The German losses were upwards of 150,000 men. On the coast the Belgians cut the dikes of the river Yser (ī′ser) and flooded the neighboring lowlands, thus putting a stop to any further advance of the enemy.

Trench Warfare. — By this time the combatants had reached a temporary deadlock. Both had adopted trench tactics, and for over three hundred miles, from the sea to the Swiss border, two systems of entrenchments paralleled one another. The trenches were protected in front by intricate networks of barbed wire. Looked at from above, the trenches seemed to be dug with little system. But they rigidly adhered to one military maxim, — that fortifications must not continue in a straight line, because such straight trenches are liable to be enfiladed from either end. Hence the trenches curve and twist, with here and there supporting trenches and supply trenches. Sometimes the trenches are covered; sometimes dugouts and caves are constructed. Every turn or corner is protected with machine-guns. In some portions of the line these trenches faced one another for over four years with scarcely any change in their relative locations.

German Treatment of Occupied Territory. — Eastward of the German trenches lay all of Belgium except a very small corner, and the richest manufacturing districts of France, including eighty per cent of the iron and steel industries, and fifty per cent of the coal. On the other hand the Allies had occupied only a small section of German territory at the southern end of the line, in Alsace.

German occupation of Belgium and northeastern France was accompanied by horrible barbarities and systematic frightfulness, which were in violation of the Hague Conventions as well as of other laws and usages of civilized warfare. The aim at first was to terrorize the people and reduce them to a condition of fear and of servility to the conquerors. Men and women were executed without adequate evidence or trial; many German soldiers were quartered in the homes; at the slightest sign of resistance innocent persons were punished for the guilty; immense fines and forced contributions were imposed upon the communities; furniture, works of art, beautiful buildings, and historic structures were ruthlessly pillaged and destroyed. In the second place, the Germans began a systematic plundering of the occupied country, taking for transportation to Germany anything they deemed useful or valuable. Nearly every article made of metal, wool, rubber, or leather was seized. Machinery from Belgian and French factories was taken to German establishments. Households were compelled to surrender bathtubs, door knobs and knockers, kitchen utensils, gas fixtures, bedclothes, etc. Food, farm animals, and farm products were confiscated; and the population was saved from actual starvation only by the energies of Belgium's friends in France, England, and America. At a later time, a third policy of the Germans was to drag Belgian and French young men and women away from their families and relatives and compel them to work far from their homes in factories, fields, and mines. Probably more than two hundred thousand persons were forced into this industrial slavery. Finally, where the Germans were forced to retire from the lands they had occupied in northern France and in Belgium, they sought to reduce much of the evacuated territory to a desert condition. Not only were bridges and roads destroyed, but houses, factories, and churches were leveled to the ground, and the foundation walls and cellars were obliterated. In some parts of France even the fruit trees and grapevines, the product of many years' growth and care, were systematically destroyed, and everything which might make the land habitable disappeared.

The War in the East.—As has already been explained, the German military leaders had counted upon a rapid crushing of France by way of Belgium before Russia should have time to complete her military preparations for attacking eastern Germany. But during the time lost through the unexpected resistance of Belgium huge Russian armies were gathered together in Russian Poland for an invasion of Germany and Austria-Hungary.

The western border of Russian Poland is less than two hundred miles from Berlin. But Russia could not advance along this road without running the risk of having the Germans from the north and the Austrians from the south cut off her armies from their sources of supply in Russia. In other words, Russia dared not advance on Berlin without first driving the Germans out of East Prussia and the Austrians from Galicia. Hence the plan of her campaign in 1914 was to invade these two provinces.

Battle of Tannenberg. — Two Russian armies entered East Prussia in the middle of August. At first they met with success. The nature of the country, however, was against them, as there was a chain of almost impassable lakes, marshes, and rivers stretching across their route. In this difficult territory they were surprised by German reinforcements which had been rushed to the east. In the battle of Tan'nenberg (August 26–31), the German troops under the command of General von Hindenburg inflicted a crushing defeat upon the

Russians, capturing 70,000 men and large quantities of supplies. Hindenburg followed up his success, and the Russians were completely expelled from East Prussia.

The Russians Overrun Galicia. — The second part of the Russian plan, the invasion of Galicia, was more successful. In September the important city of Lemberg was taken, and the fortress of Przemysl (pshem′ishl) was besieged. By December almost the whole province was in Russian hands. South of Galicia, separating it from Hungary, are the Carpathian Mountains. Russian troops penetrated the passes of this mountain wall and conducted a series of successful raids upon the plains of northern Hungary.

The Russian Situation at the Close of 1914. — At the end of the year Russia, while she had achieved success in Galicia, had failed in East Prussia. An advance toward Berlin was for the time out of the question. Indeed the Germans had themselves taken the offensive and had entered Russian Poland. In October an advance of German and Austrian troops threatened Warsaw, the most important city in Poland. The Russians in spite of strong efforts were unable to drive their enemies entirely out of this region. On the whole, therefore, the Russian situation at the end of 1914 was disappointing. Russia's accomplishment consisted of her victories in Galicia, and, probably more important, the drawing of German troops from the western front and the consequent weakening of Germany's offensive in France and Belgium. Russia was no farther on the road to Berlin than at the opening of the war.

Serbian Resistance to Austria. — An Austrian attempt to overwhelm Serbia in the first weeks of the war met with disastrous failure. This was due to two causes: (1) the brave resistance of the Serbian troops; (2) the fact that the greater part of the Austrian forces had to be used for defense against the Russian invaders of Galicia. Serbia after severe fighting compelled the Austrians to retreat beyond their own boundaries. Early in September the Serbians took the offensive and began an invasion of Austria-Hungary. This venture failed, and before long Serbia was once more resisting the enemy on her own soil. Belgrade fell into Austrian hands on December 2. It did not long remain in the possession of the conquerors. On the 14th, it was regained by the Serbians, and the Austrian armies once more expelled. The little Balkan kingdom seemed to be holding her own.

Turkey Enters the War. — In the years before the war, Germany had carefully cultivated the friendship of the Turkish government. By means of intrigue, she had practically made herself master of that country, particularly in military matters. The Turkish army had been trained by Germans, and many of its officers were Germans. Although at the opening of the war Turkey declared herself neutral, she soon showed herself an ally of the Central Powers. There is evidence to show that as early as August 4 she had entered into

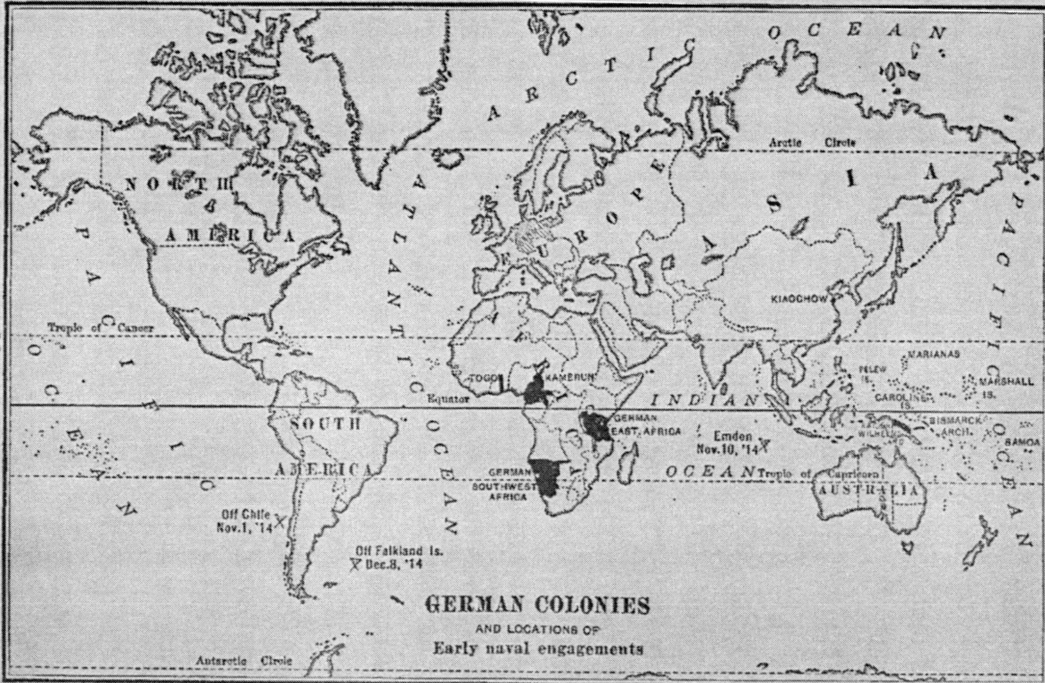

GERMAN COLONIES
AND LOCATIONS OF
Early naval engagements

a secret treaty with Germany. In October Turkey startled the world by bombarding a Russian port on the Black Sea and destroying French and Russian vessels at Odessa. These acts were regarded by Russia as acts of war. A few days later France and Great Britain declared war on Turkey.

Germany welcomed the entrance of Turkey into the war for two reasons. In the first place she expected that the Mohammedans under English and French rule, that is, those living in Morocco, Algeria, Egypt, and India, would join the Turkish Sultan, the religious head of the Mohammedan world, and engage in a "Holy War" against Great Britain and France. In this hope she was doomed to disappointment. In the second place Germany rejoiced at the arrival of a new enemy for Russia who might keep the Russians occupied along their southern borders and so weaken their efforts on other fronts.

German Colonies in the Pacific. — During the first four months of the war all of Germany's possessions in the Pacific were lost to her. On the outbreak of the war, Australia and New Zealand promptly organized expeditionary forces which attacked and captured the German colonies and coaling stations situated south of the Equator. German Samoa, the first to be taken, surrendered to the New Zealand expeditionary force August 29. The other German possessions in the South Pacific surrendered to the Australians.

England's ally, Japan, having entered the war August

23, 1914, sent an expeditionary force which captured and occupied the German islands in the North Pacific. Kiaochow (kyou′chō′), Germany's only colony in China, was captured by a combined Japanese and British force early in November.

The loss of these colonies so early in the war interfered seriously with German plans for a war on Allied commerce by fast cruisers. In the absence of German coaling stations, the only way such vessels could obtain coal during a long raiding voyage, would be by the chance capture of coal-laden vessels.

German Colonies in Africa. — During the last quarter century Germany had succeeded in getting control of considerable territory in Africa. There were few German colonists there. However, Germany hoped that the Boers, who had recently fought a war with the British and had been defeated, would attempt to regain their independence. In this case there was also the possibility of capturing Cape Colony and Rhodesia from the British. Much to the surprise and disgust of Germany, the Boers promptly showed their loyalty to Great Britain and aided in capturing the German colonies.

The struggle for Germany's African colonies continued for more than three years. Togo, a comparatively small colony, was captured by French and British troops shortly after the outbreak of the war. Under the Boer leaders, Generals Smuts and Botha, German Southwest Africa was conquered by July of 1915.

Kamerun in West Africa was freed from German forces in 1916. The final chapter in the fight for the German colonies was written in December of 1917, when an army from British South Africa, in coöperation with Belgian forces, completed the conquest of German East Africa.

Germany's Fleet. — When war was declared the German fleet, which had cost the people of Germany a billion and a half of dollars, was something less than two thirds the strength of the British fleet. Germany's task was to destroy the British fleet or to weaken it to such an extent that it could no longer protect the British trade in food and munitions from over seas, nor assure the safe transport of troops from Great Britain or her colonies to the various fronts.

The Work of the British Navy. — The British navy had two pieces of work to perform. In the first place its aim was to destroy or bottle up in port the main German fleet so that it should not be able to interfere with the British plans for the war. In the second place squadrons had to be sent out to search for and destroy German squadrons or vessels that were far from home ports at the outbreak of war or that were sent out to raid British and neutral commerce.

Coast Protection. — Both Great Britain and Germany protected their coasts by laying fields of mines in the sea so placed that they would float just under water and arranged to explode on contact with the hull of a ship. Through these mine fields carefully hidden channels gave access to the different ports. So long as ships stayed in port or inside the fields of mines they were safe from attack.

The Blockade of German Ports. — In July, 1914, the British navy had a grand review. When the review was over, the war clouds were so threatening that the vessels were not dismissed to their stations. At the beginning of the war Great Britain announced a blockade of German ports and assigned to her main fleet the task of carrying out the blockade.

The Battle of Helgoland Bight. — Hel'goland is a small island rising steeply out of the North Sea; it has an area of one fifth of a square mile. It was ceded to Germany by England about twenty years before the war. Germany had fortified it and made it a sort of German Gibraltar to protect her chief naval ports. The Bight of Helgoland is the passage about eighteen miles wide between the island and the German coast. Here a portion of the British fleet engaged in patrol or scout duty came in contact with a part of the German fleet (August 28, 1914). The arrival of four fast British battleships decided the contest. Germany lost three cruisers and two destroyers, while every British vessel returned to port, though some were badly battered.

German Commerce Raiders. — A few days before the outbreak of the war the German fleet in China slipped out of port. The cruiser "Emden" was detached for work in the Indian Ocean, and the rest of the squadron raided over the Pacific. November 1, a British squadron met the German ships near the coast of Chile. In a little over an hour two of the British ships had been sunk and the remainder fled to the south. Immediately on news of the defeat the British Admiralty sent a squadron of seven powerful ships to find and destroy the German squadron. The British vessels stopped at the Falkland Islands to coal. The next day the German ships appeared. When they saw the strength of the British squadron they vainly attempted to escape. In the battle that followed, four German vessels were sunk. Of the two that escaped one was, a few months later, interned in a United States port and about the same time the other was destroyed.

The "Emden," after separating from the other warships, cruised in the Indian Ocean for three months, and was the most destructive of the German raiders. She was finally located by an Australian cruiser. After a fight the German captain drove his vessel on the rocks to escape sinking. A lieutenant and forty men who had landed to destroy a wireless station, seized a schooner and escaped, landed on the coast of Arabia, and finally made their way back to Germany.

Naval Situation at the Close of 1914.—As a result of the activities of the Allied fleets, the German navy was shut up in port back of its mine fields, German commerce raiders had, with a few exceptions, been driven from the sea or destroyed, German merchant vessels were laid up in neutral or German ports, and the Allies were free to carry on the transport of troops, munitions, and other supplies with practically no fear of interference from the enemy. "The British ships, whether men-of-war or merchantmen, are upon the sea, the German in their ports."

Suggestions for Study. — 1. Locate Metz, Cologne, Liege, Namur, Lille, Verdun; the Meuse, the Marne, the Oise, the Aisne; Lemberg, Warsaw, Königsberg. 2. Look at a large map of Europe and by reference to the scale find out the following distances: Metz to Paris; Cologne to Paris (via Liege); Verdun to Berlin; Verdun to Strassburg; Liege to Paris; Warsaw to Berlin. What is the length of the Belgian coast-line; of the Dutch coast-line; of the Franco-German frontier? 3. Collect pictures and charts illustrative of trench warfare, and of devastated areas of Belgium and France. 4. Explain fully the influence of geography upon the campaigns of 1914. 5. Define neutrality; guarantee; treaty. 6. On an outline map of Europe indicate the countries fighting against Germany at the close of 1914. Indicate those fighting on the side of Germany at that time. Indicate the date when each of these countries entered the war. Draw a line showing the farthest German advance into France, and the farthest Russian advance into Germany and Austria (map, page 124). 7. What might have been the consequences if the Belgians had not resisted the German invasion? 8. Describe the German effort to reach the French coast in 1914. What would have been the probable consequences of its success? 9. What was the purpose of the English blockade of Germany? How did this blockade affect the rights of neutrals? Find out what the United States government did in the matter.

References. — *War Cyclopedia* (C. P. I.); *Study of the Great War* (C. P. I.); McKinley, *Collected Materials for the Study of the War; National School Service*, Vol. I, No. 3 (C. P. I.); *New York Times History of the European War.*

CHAPTER IX

THE WAR IN 1915

The Western Front. — The deadlock which existed on the western front at the close of 1914 continued with little change during the year 1915. There were indeed many contests which, on account of the men involved and the casualties, would in previous wars have been considered major engagements; but in spite of great preparations neither side was able to make much impression upon the entrenched line of the enemy. From the sea to the Swiss border two apparently impregnable lines of trenches faced each other.

German ingenuity and barbarity were shown in two new forms of warfare introduced during this year. Poison gas was first used, contrary to the terms of the Hague Conventions, against the Allied line on April 22, 1915. It brought on the most horrible forms of suffering and torture, and compelled a temporary withdrawal of the French and English from trenches near Ypres (eepr). Later, masks were used as a preventive of gas poisoning. Eventually the Allies were forced to adopt the use of poisonous gases in bombs and shells in order to fight the Germans with their own weapon. The other innovation was the "flame-thrower," an apparatus which threw a flame of burning liquid or gas far ahead of the troops. This has never been widely used by the Germans, because it proved almost as dangerous to themselves as it was to their opponents. A sharpshooter's bullet or a piece of shell might pierce the apparatus and the containers and produce dangerous results among the Germans.

The Gallipoli Campaign. — In the east the year opened with an attempt on the part of the Allies to force the Dardanelles with their fleets and take possession of the city of Constantinople. The campaign gets its name from the peninsula of Gallip'oli, the European shore of the Dardanelles. In February the campaign opened with a naval attack. The Turkish fortifications, however, were strong enough to defeat a purely naval attempt and the Allied fleets met with heavy losses. It has been stated since that had the Allies continued the attack one more day the Turks would have had to yield, as their ammunition was nearly exhausted. In April troops were landed on the peninsula to aid in the attack. The landing was accomplished at a terrible cost of life. Siege operations were then begun against the Turkish and German forces defending the peninsula. Month after month the fighting continued, but nothing worth while was accomplished. Finally, in January of the next year, the campaign was abandoned. It had cost the Allies heavily in money and lives, and its failure had lost to them the respect of the hesitating nations of southeastern Europe, Bulgaria and Greece.

The War on the Russian Border. — Along the Russian frontier also the Allied cause met with serious reverses.

The year had opened favorably with the Russians in control of most of Galicia. In March the great Galician fortress of Przemysl, which had successfully withstood the attacks of the Russians the previous autumn, was compelled to surrender.

Meanwhile, in January, Russia once more attempted to carry out the other part of her general plan, the invasion of East Prussia. The Russian troops succeeded as before in entering the coveted territory, this time crossing the troublesome lake region while the waters were frozen. Soon, however, the invaders met with a decisive defeat. In the Battle of the Mazurian Lakes, General von Hindenburg took 100,000 Russian prisoners; the number of killed and wounded Russian soldiers is said to have been 150,000. The Russians hurriedly retreated from German soil.

The time had now come for the Germans and Austrians definitely to assume the offensive. A strategic blow in Galicia imperiled the whole Russian front and compelled a general retreat of the Russian armies in Galicia and Poland. In June both Przemysl and Lemberg were recaptured by the Central Powers. By September all of Russian Poland had been conquered. Russia had lost 65,000 square miles of thickly populated territory. But the land was so thoroughly plundered by the German conquerors that many of the people died of starvation.

Bulgaria Enters the War. — The sympathies of the Bulgarian government had been with the Central Powers from the beginning of the war. Bulgaria had not forgiven the neighboring Balkan states for their treatment of her in the second Balkan war (1913). Against Serbia her feeling was particularly bitter. The Allied disaster at Gallipoli and the military successes of Germany and Austria in Poland and Galicia in the spring and summer of 1915 led the Bulgarians to believe that now was the time for them to strike. In October Bulgaria declared war upon Serbia, thus definitely taking her stand as an ally of the Central Powers.

Bulgaria's entrance into the war was followed by simultaneous invasions of Serbia from Austria and from Bulgaria. Under these blows the Serbians were crushed. Together with her neighbor and ally, brave little Montenegro, Serbia was overrun by her enemies. The cruelties inflicted upon the Serbian population by the invading Bulgars are said to have been fully as horrible as those which had taken place during the conquest of Belgium in 1914 and of Poland in 1915.

There was serious danger that the government of Greece would follow the lead of Bulgaria and also enter the war on the side of the Central Powers. This was prevented by two things. In the first place, a majority of the Greek people favored the cause of the Allies and were opposed to Bulgaria. In the second place, the Allies promptly landed an army at Salonica. Later on, they removed Constantine, the pro-German king of Greece, and placed his son Alexander upon the throne.

The East at the Close of 1915. — On the eastern front 1915 had been a year of failure. The Gallipoli campaign had been a humiliation for the Allies. The Russians had been driven from Russian Poland and from the Austrian province of Galicia. Bulgaria had joined the Central Powers, linking Austria-Hungary with Turkey. Serbia, the country whose quarrel had been the occasion of the whole world struggle, had been conquered by the enemies of the Allies.

Italy Enters the War. — In May, 1915, Italy declared war upon Austria, and more than a year later upon Germany. Her reasons for this action were: (1) her old enmity toward Austria; (2) her desire to annex the neighboring territory inhabited by Italians, but ruled by Austria; and (3) her feeling that Austria was opposed to Italian interests in the Balkans.

Italy entered the war with vigor although at a great disadvantage. When the northern Italian lands were freed from Austrian rule in 1866, Austria kept the highlands and mountain passes, from which she could easily descend upon the Italian lowlands. Now that war was begun, the Italians were compelled to force their way up the heights and against the fire from well-protected Austrian forts. Here upon the dizzy peaks of the Alps, or the icy surfaces of glaciers, or the rocky mountain sides, warfare has been more spectacular and has called for more daring and recklessness than anywhere else. Slides of rock and avalanches of ice sometimes have been the ammunition of armies. During the year the Italians made some progress and by December occupied positions well within the Austrian frontier; but no decisive battle had been fought or important city or fortress occupied.

Allied Control of the Sea. — Throughout 1915 — as in the preceding and the following years — the Allies maintained their control of the ocean. As a result of a proclamation declaring the North Sea a military area, and the more strict enforcement of the proclamation against sending contraband articles to Germany, the blockade against the Central Powers was more tightly drawn.

This seriously affected the commerce of the United States, not only with Germany but with neutral countries, such as Holland or Sweden, that could easily transship to Germany the supplies received. Neutral vessels were stopped and taken into Allied ports, there to be detained sometimes for long periods until a decision was reached as to the legality of their traffic. Moreover, the expense of this detention was laid upon the owners of the vessel and cargo. These acts brought forth a series of protests by our government against the policy of the Allies. The correspondence continued with varying results until the United States entered the war.

Forced Decrease of Neutral Trade with Germany. — Neutral countries adjoining Germany had been making huge profits by selling their food and other products to Germany, replacing their stores with material imported from over seas. As part of the preparation for a long war, the Allies blocked the renewal of neutral stocks of goods. The neutral countries complained vigorously, but they soon cut down their trade with Germany since they were no longer able to replenish their stock of food, rubber, metals, and other supplies.

Submarine Warfare. — In 1914, when the war broke out, Germany is said to have had but four seaworthy submarines. It is difficult to believe that she had so few, but it is certain that she did not have so many as either England, France, or Russia. German naval authorities were not convinced of the value of the submarine in war.

However, about a month after the war began, a German submarine torpedoed a British cruiser, and, within a few minutes, two others that had gone to assist the first. Germany, now realizing the value of the new weapon, began the construction of a numerous fleet of underwater boats, or U-boats. But against war ships, properly defended by guns and other means, they proved of little avail after all. Toward the end of the year, Admiral von Tirpitz, head of the German navy, hinted at an extension of the use of submarines to attack merchant ships.

Soon numbers of the submarines made their way to the waters surrounding the British Isles, where they torpedoed merchant vessels taking food and supplies to Great Britain and France. The vessels sunk were chiefly British, though some were neutral.

Protection against Submarines. — Large war ships were protected from submarines by keeping them in a mine-protected area until there was need for them at sea. At sea they were protected largely by the patrol and scouting operations carried on by lighter and faster vessels. To reduce the danger to merchant vessels from submarines, harbors and sea lanes were protected by mines and by great nets made of heavy wire cables. The seas in the immediate vicinity of Great Britain were patrolled by thousands of small, swift vessels constantly in search of U-boats.

Attempted Blockade of Great Britain. — In February, 1915, Germany declared a blockade of the British Isles. Under an actual blockade she would have the right to prevent neutral vessels from trading with Great Britain. But inasmuch as it was not possible to take seized neutral ships to German ports, the submarines would sink them, often without providing for the safety of the passengers and crews. The ultimate object of this course of action was so to reduce the world's shipping as to make it impossible for Great Britain to be supplied with the food or other materials that would enable her to carry on the war. This method of warfare, however, was contrary to the well established rules of international law. Against it the United States and other neutrals made vigorous protests.

The Lusitania. — The most notable loss by submarine attack was that of the "Lusitania," sunk without warning off the coast of Ireland on May 7, 1915. Nearly twelve hundred lives were lost, including many women and children. One hundred and fourteen of those lost were Americans. An advertisement had been inserted in the papers warning passengers not to travel on Allied ships, but no one believed that Germany would go so far in violation of international law as to torpedo, without warning, a passenger vessel carrying civilians of neutral as well as of warring nations. The people of the whole civilized world were horrified by the deed. Germany's attitude is shown by the fact that medals were struck commemorating the act, and the commander of the submarine was rewarded.

President Wilson wrote a series of notes to the German government insisting that Germany conduct her warfare in accordance with international law. This resulted in a promise by the German minister to the United States, that liners would not be sunk by German submarines without warning and without safety to the lives of noncombatants, provided that the liners did not try to escape or offer resistance.

Raids on Coast Towns. — Several times in 1914 German vessels managed to escape through the cordon of Allied ships. They proceeded to the east coast of England and bombarded defenseless fishing ports and watering places such as Yarmouth, Whitby, and Scarborough. These raids had no military effect, but they resulted in the killing or wounding of hundreds of women, children, and old men. They were undertaken for the purpose of terrorizing the civilian population of England in order to arouse a desire for peace. In January, 1915, a German squadron attempting a similar raid was intercepted and defeated by British war ships.

Zeppelins. — At the outset Germany had great faith in the usefulness of her immense dirigible balloons, or Zep'pelins, as they are commonly called. In the attack on Belgium, they were used for observation, incidentally dropping a few bombs on Antwerp. Early in 1915, Zeppelins made their appearance over England, bombing many of the smaller towns and villages, as well as London. Such raids might have some effect on the war if they were directed toward munition plants, railway stations, or naval depots. The Germans, however, generally contented themselves with attacks on defenseless residential towns and cities. Up to October, 1917, there were thirty-four such raids, resulting in the death of nearly one thousand persons and the wounding of three times as many. The result on the military situation was practically zero, except to increase the British determination to see the war through.

Later the protection afforded Great Britain by anti-aircraft guns and especially by airplanes, made it highly dangerous for Zeppelins to continue their raids. Many of them were destroyed. The later raids were made by squadrons of airplanes which had greater chances of escape. German air raiders found it increasingly difficult to get past the defenses, and in 1918 the raids on England became infrequent.

Allied Retaliation. — For a long time the Allies refused to retaliate by bombing unfortified towns in Germany, but finally they decided to do so. The immediate results were a protest from Germany that the Allies were violating international law, and a petition to the German authorities from the towns in western Germany, asking that air raids on places not in the military area should be stopped, so that the German cities should not be bombed in retaliation. Nearly all such Allied air raids, however, were directed against railroads, munition factories, and other objects of military importance.

The Allies Organize for a Long War. — When Lord Kitchener, the great British general, predicted that the war would last at least three years, hardly any one believed him. It was thought that the cost of a modern war would be so great that nations would not be able to stand the strain for more than a few months. When the Allies realized that Kitchener was right, they prepared for a long struggle. The munition factories in all the countries were reorganized, and the output of war material was increased many fold, more being produced in a few days than had formerly been produced in a year. Great Britain and France appointed ministers of munitions whose sole work was to see that the armies were supplied with guns, ammunition, and other fighting needs.

The people in the British overseas dominions remained loyal, and sent hundreds of thousands of soldiers to the battle fronts in order to protect the mother country from threatened defeat. To secure still greater coöperation throughout the British Empire, the prime ministers of the self-governing colonies were invited to places in the British imperial war conferences.

Suggestions for Study. — 1. Locate Przemysl, Lemberg, the Mazurian Lakes, Scarborough, Helgoland, Essen. 2. On an outline map of Europe indicate the countries engaged in the war at the end of 1915. Which of these countries had entered during the year? 3. By use of the scale on your map of Europe determine the following distances: Ostend to Scarborough; Berlin to Warsaw; Brussels to Paris. 4. When did the kingdom of Poland pass out of existence? What became of it? 5. What was the purpose of the Allies in the Gallipoli campaign? What would have been the consequences of the success of this campaign? 6. Collect pictures of Zeppelins, of gas attacks, and of methods of defense against gas.

References. — *War Cyclopedia* (C. P. I.); *Study of the Great War* (C. P. I.); *New York Times History of the European War;* McKinley, *Collected Materials for the Study of the War; German War Practices* (C. P. I.), parts I and II.

CHAPTER X

THE WAR IN 1916

"They Shall Not Pass!" — Early in 1916 the Germans began a furious attack on the strong French position at Verdun. This point was a highly important one for the French, because if it were captured by the enemy, he could make flank attacks upon their adjoining lines and perhaps compel a general retreat. The Germans had long been massing materials and men for the greatest military offensive which the world had ever seen. Twenty thousand men were placed on each mile of the front for a distance of twenty-five miles, while hundreds of thousands more were held in reserve. Thousands of guns of all sizes were brought up for the attack. Under the command of the German crown prince, the German people and the whole world were to be shown that the German army was still invincible.

Beginning on February 21, the titanic struggle around Verdun continued until July, when the attacks and counter-attacks were gradually suspended. In the early attacks the French were driven in from advanced positions, and then the Germans charged the heavily protected woodlands and hills. In massed formation they advanced in the face of artillery, machine-gun, and rifle fire of the heaviest character. The first waves were mown down like grain; but other troops, and still others climbed over the bodies of their dead comrades. Never since the world began had such slaughter been seen.

During the intervals between the infantry attacks the French troops were subjected to an unprecedented artillery fire. Suffering under a strain such as armies had never hitherto known, the French patriots yet held true to their watchword,—"They shall not pass." General Pétain (pā-tăn'), in a stirring address, said to his entrenched heroes, "Courage, we'll get them!" ("*Courage, on les aura!*"), and this phrase became the Verdun battle-cry. Try as the Germans would, from every possible point, they could not break through the living wall of Frenchmen. A little ground was won here and there, but before the end of the year nearly all had been retaken by the French. At a frightful cost the German crown prince and his military advisers had put their fighting machine to the test, and it had failed. A half million men, killed, wounded, or prisoners, were lost to the Germans before they ceased their attacks at this point.

The Battle of the Somme.—In July, 1916, while the Verdun struggle was still undetermined, the French and British troops began an advance on the German line along the river Somme (som). Exceedingly heavy artillery attacks first battered down the enemy defenses, and then the infantry went "over the top." During the long course of the Battle of the Somme (July 1 to November 17) the Allies advanced on a front of twenty miles to a maximum depth of about nine miles. Slowly, and at great expense of ammunition and men on both sides, the Allied progress had been won. They had failed to break through the German line, but they had shown how it might gradually be pushed back. And they had relieved the important position of Verdun from further severe attacks, because German forces were needed to the westward.

In the course of this battle, on September 15, the British first used their most original military machines — the "tanks." Thereafter these armored cruisers of the land were to play an increasingly important part along the western front.

Increased Use of Aircraft. — Aircraft, too, were every day becoming more valuable. In the first year of the war airplanes were used mainly for observation purposes: to find the location of enemy forts, trenches, troops, and batteries; and to direct the fire of the aviator's own batteries. Hundreds of photographs were taken by the airmen, rapidly developed, and within thirty minutes the staff officers could be seen studying them with microscopes to determine what changes had taken place within the enemy's lines. Anchored balloons, too, were used for similar purposes.

Airplane construction and use developed more rapidly than any other feature in the war. After the observation machines, came the battle-planes, whose first purpose was to clear the way and protect the observation planes. Later, heavy machines for bombing expeditions were constructed; and squadrons of airplanes now took part in every battle, preceding the attacking party, and firing with machine-guns and bombs upon the enemy's trenches or his massed troops back of the line.

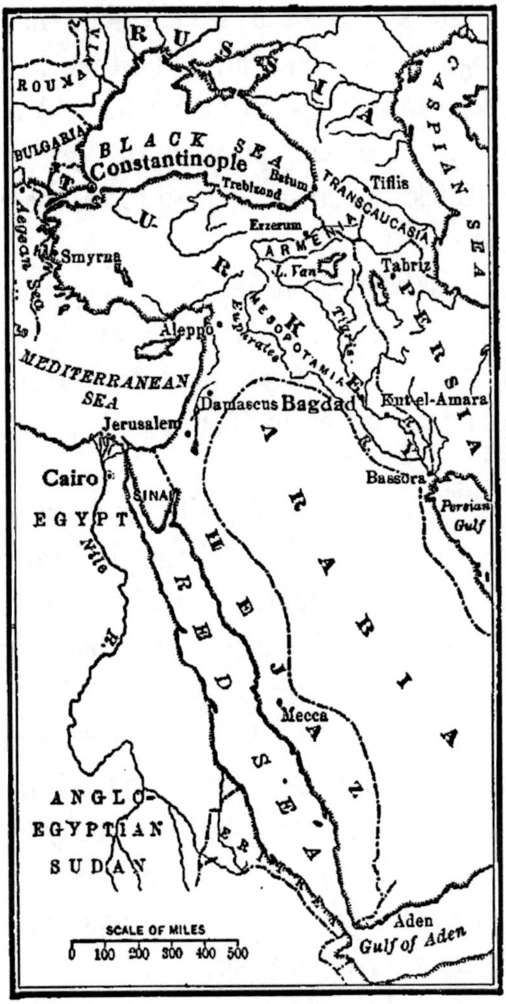

The Russians Invade Turkey in Asia.—In the early months of 1916 Russian troops met with success in an offensive in the part of Turkey south of the Caucasus. This territory, known as Arme′nia, is inhabited by a Christian population who for many years had been the victims of Turkish persecutions; half a million were cruelly exterminated after Turkey allied herself with Germany in 1914. The Russians advanced steadily, inflicting serious defeats upon the Turkish forces.

In February they took possession of Erz′erum, a strongly fortified city of Armenia. The capture of this point was of importance because it was a step in the plan for coöperation with the British armies which were pushing their way north from the region of the Persian Gulf. It had the further important result of interrupting Turkish plans for an invasion of Egypt by way of the Isthmus of Suez, as Turkey was compelled to concentrate her power for the defense of her own territory.

In April, Treb′izond, the most important city on the Turkish shore of the Black Sea, surrendered to the invading Russian army. The Russians, supported by fleets along the coast, had made the defense of the city impossible. The fall of Trebizond was a very serious blow to the power of Turkey in Asia Minor.

The Campaign in Mesopotamia. — Part of the Allied plan in the east was for the junction of Russian armies operating from the region of the Caucasus with British troops from the land around the Persian Gulf. While the Russians, as we have seen, were making a noteworthy success of their part of this program, the British had not been so fortunate. Their plan was to take possession of Mesopotamia, the valley of the Tigris-Euphrates, and occupy its capital, the famous city of Bagdad. General Townshend with an insufficient force had begun his march up the Tigris River the year before and in March, 1915, had occupied the stronghold of Kut-el-Ama′ra, about 100 miles below Bagdad. Here later he was besieged by a Turkish army. A Russian army on the way from Erzerum and an English relief force from the south failed to reach the place in time, and April 29, 1916, General Townshend was forced by starvation to surrender.

Russian Successes in Austria. — During the summer months the Russians under the command of one of their greatest leaders, General Bru′silov, renewed their offensive against the border lands of Austria-Hungary. It looked for a while as if the disasters of 1915 in this region were about to be redeemed. On a wide front extending from the Prip′et marshes in eastern Poland all the way to Bukowina (boo-ko-vee′nah), the Austrian province southeast of Galicia, the Russian armies advanced. They invaded Galicia and took hundreds of thousands of Austrian prisoners. Austria was compelled to transfer troops from her Italian front. The year 1916 closed with the Russians in a decidedly more favorable military position than they had occupied a year before.

Roumania in the War. — Roumania had long looked forward to an extension of her boundaries to include all the Roumanians of southeastern Europe. Across the border, in southeastern Hungary, were more than two million Roumanians living in the large region known as Transylvania. The annexation of Transylvania was one of the greatest ambitions of Roumanian leaders. In August, 1916, encouraged by the promises of Russia, her powerful neighbor and protector, Roumania entered the war on the side of the Allies.

On her western front Roumania could easily defend herself from invasion because of strong mountain barriers. Her point of danger was the Bulgarian boundary between the Danube and the Black Sea. Here she should have concentrated her strength for defense against the Bulgarian forces or even for an offensive into Bulgaria. Instead she sent most of her armies west into Transylvania. Presently a strong force of Germans and Bulgarians crossed the border into southeastern Roumania (the Dobrudja) and marched north in a resistless offensive. Meanwhile the Roumanians in Transylvania, far from their base of supplies, had advanced too fast for safety. Moreover, they suffered from a shortage of ammunition, probably caused by the failure of certain pro-German Russian officials to coöperate with the Roumanians as they had promised. A large German army attacked the Roumanian forces and drove them back with heavy losses to their own borders. The boundaries were then crossed by the invaders and the greater part of the country occupied. This disaster brought enormous advantages to the enemy. The battle front of the Central Powers was shortened by five hundred miles, the oil and wheat fields which constitute the chief wealth of Roumania fell into their hands, and their communications with Turkey were materially strengthened.

The Italian Front. — The winter of 1915–1916 was uncommonly severe in the Alps; snow thirty feet deep lay on some of the passes, and military operations were brought almost to a standstill. During the spring the Austrians made preparations for a great offensive against Italy, collecting over a third of a million of men and enormous stores of provisions and munitions. During May and June, 1916, this Austrian force drove back the Italians from their advanced positions in the Trentino valley. It seemed that the enemy would enter the valley of the Po and capture the cities of the most prosperous part of Italy. But the farther the Austrian army advanced, the more difficult it was to bring supplies up the narrow Alpine valleys. Meantime, on the eastern frontier the Russians began their great drive into Austrian territory. There was nothing for the Austrians to do but retire from the Trentino front. This they did with the loss of one third of their force, and of great quantities of war material.

The Italians now took the offensive, not only on the Trentino, but also on their eastern frontier, where, the year before, they had begun an advance toward the "unredeemed" territory around Trieste (map, page 50). The Ison'zo River was crossed and after months of warfare the city and fortresses of Gorizia (go-rit'si-a) were occupied (August 9, 1916). From this point the Italians continued slowly, overcoming great difficulties, on their way toward Trieste.

The Battle of Jutland, May 31, 1916. — A minor division of the British fleet under Admiral Beatty was scouting in the neighborhood of Jutland (the peninsula of Denmark). The main German fleet came out to attack it. The small British squadron, instead of withdrawing, gave battle to the whole German high seas fleet. After the fighting had gone on for several hours in fog and mist, the British grand fleet approached, but night came on before a decision was reached. During the night the German fleet retired back of the defenses of mines and shore batteries. In the battle the British fleet had lost three battle cruisers and fifteen or sixteen other vessels. The German losses were not completely published but were certainly heavier. The Germans claimed a victory, and a general holiday was ordered that all might celebrate. Nevertheless, the British vessels were on the scene the next morning picking up survivors, while the German fleet has not (up to the present writing) come out of harbor in order that it might try to repeat its so-called victory.

Submarine Warfare. — During the year 1916 Germans continued with increasing success their policy of sinking merchant vessels, neutral and enemy. Out of a total of nearly 4,000,000 tons of shipping destroyed from the beginning of the war to January 1, 1917, more than half was lost during 1916. Occasional loss of life also caused much doubt on the part of our government as to whether Germany was keeping her pledge to safeguard the lives of noncombatants on torpedoed liners.

When a passenger steamer, the "Sussex," plying between England and France, was torpedoed without warning (March 24, 1916), eighty of the passengers were killed or injured, two of the latter being Americans.

Germany at first said that one of her submarines had torpedoed a vessel in the vicinity, but not the "Sussex." The finding of fragments of a German torpedo on the "Sussex" after it was brought into port conclusively proved that the Germans were responsible, and that Germany had broken her promise. President Wilson addressed a note to the German government, stating that he would sever diplomatic relations with it unless Germany should both declare and effect an abandonment of her unlawful methods of submarine warfare. Thereupon the German government gave a written pledge that merchant ships "shall not be sunk without warning and without saving human lives, unless these ships attempt to escape or offer resistance." This pledge was given on the condition that the United States should demand that Great Britain observe certain (disputed) rules of international law; but our government refused to agree that Germany's respect for our neutral rights should be made to depend on the conduct of other nations. President Wilson thus made clear his intention to sever diplomatic relations if Germany's pledge should be withdrawn or violated.

Conscription in Great Britain.—The British government had kept up its army by volunteering. The need of an army of five million could not depend on this plan. A conscription bill therefore was passed making all males between certain ages liable for military service. Ireland was excepted from the provisions of this act.

Sinn Fein Rebellion.—Some of the more radical

among the Irish Home Rule party had formed an organization known as the Sinn Fein (shin fān), an Irish phrase which means "for ourselves." Their aim was to make Ireland an independent nation. The leaders of this group got into correspondence with persons in Germany and were promised military assistance if they would rebel against England. The rebellion broke out April 24, 1916, without the promised help from Germany. For several days the rebels held some of the principal buildings in Dublin. After much bloodshed the rebellion was put down, and Sir Roger Casement, one of those who had been in communication with Germany, was executed for treason.

Suggestions for Study. — 1. On an outline map of Europe indicate the countries engaged in the war at the end of 1916. Indicate the date of the entrance of each and the side on which it was fighting. 2. Collect pictures illustrative of life in the Balkans and of the war in that region. 3. Locate Armenia. What do you know of the race and religion of its population? 4. Where is Bagdad? Why is it important for the British Empire that the valley of the Tigris-Euphrates should not fall into the possession of a strong hostile power? What do you know of the history of this region in ancient times? What may become of Mesopotamia at the close of the war? 5. In regard to Roumania tell what you know of its race, language, religion, and industries prior to the war. Compare this country with Bulgaria in regard to the facts you have mentioned.

References. — *War Cyclopedia* (C. P. I.); *Study of the Great War* (C. P. I.); McKinley, *Collected Materials for the Study of the War; New York Times History of the European War.*

CHAPTER XI

THE WAR IN 1917

The Western Front. — During the winter of 1916–1917 there was little infantry warfare in France, although the heavy guns kept up their cannonades. In the spring of 1917 the Allies planned a great drive on the enemy positions in the valley of the Somme. But in March the Germans began a general retirement to a more easily defended line — the so-called Hindenburg line — on a front of one hundred miles, from Arras (ạr-rahss′) to Soissons (swah-sawn′).[1] Completely destroying the villages, churches, castles, vineyards, and orchards, they left a desolate waste behind them. In this retreat the Germans gave up French territory to the extent of thirteen hundred square miles.

The German retirement was closely followed by British and French troops. Great courage was shown by Canadian troops in the taking of Vimy Ridge on April 9. In the following month many attacks were made by the British and French, which resulted in the taking of nearly 50,000 prisoners and large quantities of munitions, and the breaking through the Hindenburg line in one place. During the summer and fall the Allied attacks continued to win small territorial gains. The artillery

[1] The Hindenburg line was very nearly the same as the battle line of Jan. 1, 1918, as shown on the map, page 145.

fire was very heavy during all this time. During a period of three weeks the French city of Rheims (reemz or rănss) alone, with its magnificent cathedral almost in ruins, was bombarded with 65,000 large caliber German shells.

Two very important ridges, from which artillery could reach German positions, were taken during the heavy fighting in November. The French forced a retreat of the Germans over a thirteen-mile front and occupied the ridge known as Chemin des Dames (shmăn dā dahm); while the Canadians secured Passchendaele (pahss-ken-dĕl′ā) Ridge.

Late in the year the British introduced a new method of warfare. Instead of beginning their attack with a great bombardment lasting many hours and thus indicating to the enemy the approximate time and place of attack, they sent over the front a large number of "tanks" which broke through the barbed wire entanglements and opened the way for the infantry. By this means the British successfully surprised the enemy in the battle of Cambrai (cahn-brĕ′; November 20 to December 13). Unfortunately they could not hold most of the land occupied, — which was lost later in the battle, — but they did show the possibility of breaking the old deadlock of trench fighting. The new method was to be used by both sides during the campaigns of the following year.

The War in the Air. — During this year warfare in the air continued to advance. Guynemer (geen-mĕr′), the great French ace, who was lost on September 11, had to his credit the destruction of fifty-four enemy machines. The increase in the number of airplanes led to the grouping of large numbers into regular formations (escadrilles), sometimes composed of over a hundred planes. Each year showed a steady increase in the effectiveness of this kind of warfare. In 1916 a total of 611 enemy machines had been destroyed or damaged by the Allied forces. In 1917 the French destroyed forty-three in twenty-four hours; and the British brought down thirty-one enemy planes in one combat. In a single week in 1918 the Allies destroyed 339 German planes. On one day, October 9, 1918, three hundred and fifty airplanes were sent forth by the American army in a single bombing expedition.

The Russian Revolution. — In 1917 the Allied cause received a heavy blow through the collapse of the Russian government. Long before the war there had been parties in Russia which desired to do away with the autocratic government of the Czar and substitute some sort of representative system which would give to the people a voice in the management of their affairs. These reforming parties did not agree among themselves as to the kind of government they wished to set up; their ideas extended from limited monarchy of the English type, all the way to anarchy, which means no government at all. In 1905 the Czar met the wishes of the reformers to the extent of establishing the Duma, a sort of representative assembly or parliament, which should help in making the laws. The Duma, however, was never given any real authority, and as time passed those who believed in Russian democracy became more and more dissatisfied.

During the war the Germans by means of bribery and plotting did all they could to weaken the authority of the Russian government. There existed, moreover, much corruption and disloyalty among high Russian officials. As the war dragged on a shortage of food added to the general discontent. By the early months of 1917, conditions were very bad indeed, and dissatisfied crowds gathered in the streets of Petrograd. Hunger and hardship had made them desperate, and they refused to disperse until the government should do something to relieve the situation. Regiments of soldiers were summoned to fire upon the crowd. They refused to do so and finally joined the mob. Thus began the Russian Revolution.

At a meeting of the revolutionists a group of soldiers and working men was selected to call upon the Duma and ask that body to form a temporary government. Another committee was sent to inform Nicholas II that he was deposed. Messages were sent to the armies to notify the generals that there was no longer a Russian Empire and that they were to take their orders thereafter from the representatives of the Russian people. Within a few days the revolution was complete. On March 15, the Czar signed a paper giving up the throne of Russia. Moderate reformers were placed in charge of the different departments of the government. The new government was recognized by the United States, Great Britain, France, and Italy. It looked as if the revolution had established a free government for Russia and that thenceforth, as a democratic nation, she would fight better than ever by the side of her allies. In all the Russian provinces, elections were called for choosing delegates to an assembly that should make a new constitution for Russia.

Russia under Kerensky. — Meanwhile the extreme socialists began at once to make trouble for the new government. These men for the most part owned no property and wanted all wealth equally divided among the entire population. They considered the new government as tyrannical as that of the Czar had been. They also favored an immediate peace. Chief among the moderate leaders during this period was Alexander Keren'sky. He saw the necessity of keeping the revolution within bounds. For a while he was strong enough to maintain a moderate government in spite of the opposition of the extreme socialists. The Germans, meanwhile, through spies and secret agents, had been spreading among the Russian soldiers the idea that Germany was really their friend and that it was to their interest to stop fighting and retreat. Kerensky personally visited the battle front in Galicia, and for a time by means of his rousing speeches to the soldiers kept up their fighting spirit. New advances were made, the Germans and Austrians being driven back many miles.

Lemberg itself seemed about to fall once more into the hands of the Russians. But this success was only temporary. Owing to the shortage of ammunition and the rapid spread of peace sentiments among the troops, the Russian army became disorganized and retreated from Galicia.

The Bolsheviki. — Bolsheviki (bōl-shĕv′e-kee) is the name given to the extreme socialistic party in Russia. From the beginning they had opposed the control of affairs by the moderate revolutionists under Kerensky. At last, in the fall of 1917, helped by the depression caused by the German advance and by the strikes and food riots which once more broke out in the capital, they succeeded in winning over to their side the Petrograd garrison and the navy, and drove Kerensky from the city (November 7). Their revolt was led by two of the most extreme members of the party, Lenine and Trotzky, who had at their disposal large sums of money furnished by Germany.

No sooner were the Bolsheviki in control than they announced themselves in favor of an immediate peace. They proclaimed that all the land should at once be divided among the peasants. When the new representative assembly met to make a constitution, it was found to be too moderate to suit the Bolshevik leaders, who dispersed it before it could accomplish anything. The rule of Lenine and Trotzky promised to be even more tyrannical than anything that had preceded it in Russia.

Meanwhile the Bolsheviki had arranged for an armistice with Germany with a view toward immediate negotiations for peace. This arrangement for the cessation of military operations became effective December 7. In spite of its provisions, however, the Germans, who had taken Riga (ree′ga) in September, continued their advance into Russian territory. By the close of

1917 peace negotiations were in progress between Russia and her enemies. Russia under Bolshevik control had definitely deserted her allies.

The British in Mesopotamia. — It will be remembered that the Allied war plans in 1916 had included the junction of Russian armies operating from the Caucasus with British troops advancing north from the Persian Gulf. After the disaster at Kut-el-Amara the British still held the territory about the mouth of the Tigris. In January, 1917, they began a new advance up the river in the direction of Bagdad. This time their efforts proved successful. In February, Kut-el-Amara was retaken from the Turks, and on March 11 the British entered the city of Bagdad. They also continued their advance a considerable distance along the Bagdad Railway and occupied much of the Euphrates valley.

Still more important victories would probably have resulted from this campaign had it not been for the outbreak of the Russian revolution. This had the effect of weakening Russian military coöperation, and finally of removing Russia entirely from the war, leaving to Great Britain alone the task of dealing with the Turkish armies in Asia. But the British kept their hold on the city of Bagdad, thus checkmating the German scheme of a Berlin-Bagdad railway and protecting India from any offensive on this side.

The Palestine Campaign. — The year 1917 witnessed still another military success for the British in Asia. The Turks had made several attempts to seize the

Suez Canal and so inflict a serious blow against the communications of the Allies with the Far East. To remove, if possible, the danger of further threats against this vital spot, the English at last decided upon an offensive in that region. Early in 1917, the British advance began. During January and February important positions on the Sinai peninsula were seized. This success was followed by a slow progress north into Palestine. The resistance of the Turks was powerful and the British met with serious reverses. The terrible heat of the summer months further held up their operations. In the fall, however, the advance was resumed and a number of towns in the Holy Land fell into the hands of the British. In November, Jaffa, the seaport of Jerusalem, was taken. All the Turkish positions around the Holy City were carried by storm, and on December 10 Jerusalem surrendered to General Allenby.

This successful campaign in Palestine had several important results. The capture of Jerusalem after almost seven centuries of Turkish control led to general rejoicing among the Allied nations. Large numbers of Jews throughout the world, who had long looked forward to the reëstablishment of a Jewish nation in Palestine, now felt that a long step had been taken toward the realization of their hopes. From a military point of view, however, the chief result of the British campaign in Palestine was that it definitely freed the Suez Canal from further danger of a Turkish attack.

The Offensive against Italy. — At the beginning of 1917 the Italian forces were within eleven miles of their great objective, the city and port of Trieste. During the late spring and summer the advance continued. Austrian trenches were occupied and tens of thousands of Austrian soldiers were captured. After two years of effort it seemed that the Italians would obtain the city and incorporate its population — very largely Italian — into the kingdom of Italy. But conditions in Austria and Germany had greatly changed. The cessation of war by Russia relieved the Central Powers of the necessity of keeping large armies on the eastern front. Further, the campaign had been going against Germany on the western front, and an easy victory in Italy might quiet criticism at home.

An immense army of Austrians and Germans was gathered together to attack the Italian forces. The Italians were spread out in a semicircle about one hundred and fifty miles long stretching from near Trent to within a few miles of Trieste. The Austrians controlled the upper passes in the mountains, so that they could attack this long line where they would. Thus the Italian military position was difficult to defend. The campaign began with a surprise attack by picked German troops at a point where the morale of one Italian division had previously been weakened by the pretended fraternizing of Austrian troops.

The Austro-German drive (October–December, 1917) swiftly undid the work of two years of most arduous endeavor. The Italians were forced back from Gorizia and compelled to surrender mountain positions which had been captured by them at enormous cost. Back across the boundary they retreated, losing heavily in men and material. The enemy advanced into the low country near Venice, and it seemed for a time that the city would fall into their hands. But British and French assistance was sent to Italy, the Italian army recovered its spirit, and a permanent check was put to the enemy's advance before Venice was reached. Upon a much shorter but more defensible line the Italians held the enemy at bay in the mountains and along the river Piave (pyäh'vā).

Unrestricted Submarine Warfare. — On January 31, 1917, the German ambassador to the United States, Count von Bernstorff, announced to President Wilson that Germany would begin unrestricted submarine warfare the following day, in the waters around Great Britain and France,[1] thus withdrawing the pledge given as a result of

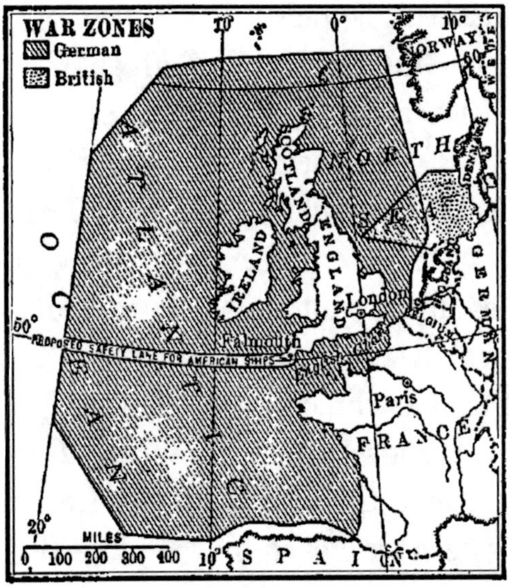

[1] Except that the United States, on certain conditions, might send one ship a week to Falmouth.

the sinking of the "Sussex." Three days later the President handed Count von Bernstorff his passports and recalled Ambassador Gerard' from Berlin, thus severing diplomatic relations with Germany.

During the next six months shipping was sunk at an average rate of 600,000 tons per month, three times as fast as before, and two or three times faster than it was being replaced. The highwater mark was reached in April, when 800,000 tons of shipping were destroyed. Unless this loss could be greatly reduced the Allies for want of food and materials would soon have to give up fighting.

But methods were quickly devised to combat the new danger. The patrols were increased, ships voyaged under convoy of fast destroyers constantly hovering about on the watch for submarines, and other protective measures were taken, so that the submarine menace was soon much reduced. By September, 1918, the sinkings were only about 150,000 tons a month, while the production of ships, especially in the United States, has increased to several times this amount.

Apparently Germany had waited until she had built a large number of submarines, thinking that by the use of a great fleet of them in a ruthless warfare on shipping she could force a peace within a few months. In this expectation she was disappointed. The principal result of the withdrawal of her pledge to this country was the entrance of the United States into the war on the side of the Allies. Captain Persius, an expert

German naval critic, admitted in November, 1917, that the German admiralty was grossly mistaken in its calculations and that Germany had no reason for believing in the decisive influence of the submarine war.

The United States Drifts toward War. — The breaking off of diplomatic relations is not a declaration of war. Nevertheless the events immediately succeeding the withdrawal of Count von Bernstorff made a declaration of war increasingly probable. The most important of these were the publication of the Zimmerman note, the fact that several American merchant ships were actually sunk by German submarines, and the discovery that members of the German embassy and other German diplomatic representatives had been concerned in plotting on United States soil against the Allies, thus endangering our peaceful relations with them. Not only so, but there was evidence that plots had been laid to destroy American lives and property in this country and to stir up internal disorders, such as strikes and riots.

The Zimmerman Note. — On the last day of February, the Secretary of State published a note that had come into his possession which was addressed by Dr. Zimmerman, the German foreign minister, to the German minister in Mexico. The note stated that Germany would soon begin a ruthless submarine warfare and proposed, if the United States should declare war on Germany, that Mexico should enter into an alliance with Germany. Germany was to furnish money and Mexico was to reconquer New Mexico, Texas, and Arizona. It was also hinted that Mexico should suggest to Japan that the latter country should come into the agreement. The interesting thing about the note is that it was dated January 19, twelve days before Germany announced to us her plan for ruthless submarine warfare, and during a time when our relations with Germany, though under a great strain, were still peaceable.

Armed Neutrality. — About the time the Zimmerman note was published, President Wilson asked Congress to authorize the arming of American merchant ships for their own defense. A small minority in Congress by their obstructive tactics prevented the passage of the desired resolution before Congress expired on March 4. On March 12 the President announced that this country had determined to place an armed guard on all United States merchant vessels, which under international law might defend themselves from attack, although Germany denied this right. There is no evidence, however, that there was any encounter between these armed ships and German vessels prior to the outbreak of the war.

The President's War Message. — When Russia deposed the Czar and established a democratic government, in March, 1917, the last reason was removed which might have held us back from a declaration of war. Many believed that it would have been illogical for us to fight for democracy side by side with one of the greatest of autocracies. President Wilson called Congress in special session and on April 2 delivered his famous war message, asking Congress to declare that a state of war existed between the United States and Germany.

In the message he told of the various acts of Germany which had led up to the verge of war, recited the steps which our government had taken to bring Germany to realize the inevitable results of her crimes against civilization, and concluded by asking Congress to declare war. The President stated that the aims of the United States in the war are:

1. That the people of every nation may determine the form of government under which they wish to live.

2. That the small nations may have the right to exist and be protected against aggression.

3. That the future peace of the world may be guaranteed through the formation of a league of nations.

4. That the world may be made safe for democracy.

The Declaration of War. — In accordance with the recommendation of the President, Congress declared war against Germany on April 6, 1917. War was not declared at this time against Germany's allies, Austria, Turkey, and Bulgaria. A few days later, however, at the instance of Germany, Austria and Turkey broke off diplomatic relations. On December 7, 1917, the United States declared war on Austria-Hungary.

Following the declaration of war with Germany, steps were at once taken to put the country in a position to give effective aid to our associates, and the President from time to time has requested Congress to grant authority to do those things that would enable us to take an active part in the war.

Other Countries Enter the War. — After the United States entered the war, many other countries, especially Brazil and some of the Spanish American countries, either broke off relations with Germany or declared war against her. Most of these countries had close commercial relationships with the United States, which would have been seriously interfered with had they remained neutral.

Spurlos Versenkt. — The decision of some of the South American countries to side against Germany was probably hastened by a typical piece of German bad faith. Argentina was at peace with Germany. In spite of that fact, the German minister at Buenos Aires (the Argentine capital) telegraphed to his government that if possible Argentine ships should be spared, but if not, they should be sunk without leaving a trace ("*spurlos versenkt*)." This would involve the drowning or murdering of the crews, so that there would be no inconvenient protest on the part of the Argentine government. It should be added that at the request of the German minister, the Swedish minister at Buenos Aires sent these dispatches in code as if they were his own private messages. In this way the German minister was able to have them sent over cable lines controlled by the Allies.

Suggestions for Study. — 1. What is a "tank"? What are small tanks called? 2. Define socialism; Bolsheviki. 3. On a map of Europe show Germany and her allies in black. Mark with black lines other territory held or controlled by the Central Powers at the close of 1917. 4. On a map of southern Europe show Italy's farthest advance into Austrian territory in 1917. 5. Collect pictures of Rheims Cathedral, before and after being bombarded by the Germans; also pictures of other places destroyed by bombardments. Get pictures of different sorts of tanks and airplanes, of destroyers and Eagle boats. 6. What was the object of the Germans in devastating the country when they retreated to the Hindenburg line? 7. Why did Germany think Mexico and Japan might join her in an attack on the United States? 8. What was the date on which the United States declared war on Germany? 9. Why did not the United States declare war on Turkey or Bulgaria? 10. Make a list of the countries of South America and Central America that declared war on Germany.

References. — *War Cyclopedia* (C. P. I.); *The Study of the Great War* (C. P. I.); *War, Labor, and Peace* (C. P. I.); *How the War came to America* (C. P. I.); *The War Message and the Facts Behind It* (C. P. I.); *New York Times History of the European War.*

CHAPTER XII

THE WAR IN 1918

Failure of German Peace Offensive. — During the fall of 1917 Germany had started a great discussion of the terms of the peace which should close the war. In general the position taken by German spokesmen was "peace without annexations and without indemnities," as proposed by the Russian Bolsheviki. Such talk was designed to weaken the war spirit of the Allied peoples, and perhaps to make the German people believe that they were fighting a war of self-defense. The time was ripe for a statement of the war aims of Germany's opponents. This statement, later approved in general by Allied statesmen, was made by President Wilson in his address to Congress on January 8, 1918. It is discussed in detail in Chapter XIV. It was not satisfactory to Germany's rulers, for they hoped to secure better terms in a peace of bargains and compromises.

Russia Makes a Separate Peace. — Only in Russia was this German peace offensive a success. In the last chapter we saw how in the latter part of 1917 the Bolsheviki had gained control of the government of Russia and had arranged an armistice with the Central Powers. This meant the stopping of all fighting along the eastern front and the consequent freeing of many thousands of German soldiers to fight in the west.

At Brest-Litovsk, a town in Russian Poland which had been occupied by the troops of the Central Powers, a meeting of delegates was called to arrange the terms of peace. The negotiations at this place lasted from December 23, 1917, to February 10, 1918. The Germans had determined to keep large portions of Russian territory. At the conference the German delegates flatly refused to promise to withdraw their troops from the occupied parts of Russia after the peace. By February 10 hope of any settlement that would satisfy Russia had disappeared and the Bolshevik delegates left Brest-Litovsk. The war, so far as Russia was concerned, was at an end, but no treaty of peace had been signed. The Bolshevik government issued orders for the complete demobilization of the Russian armies on all the battle fronts.

Germany, determined to compel Russia to accept her terms, renewed her military operations on February 18. The result was that Lenine and Trotzky, the Bolshevik leaders, were forced to agree to the conditions which had been laid down by the Central Powers at Brest-Litovsk. Nevertheless the Germans continued their advance, with practically no opposition, to within seventy miles of Petrograd.

The Separation of Ukrainia and Finland. — Ukrainia, the southwestern corner of Russia, is the home of a Slavic people — the Little Russians — closely akin to the Russians proper. The people of Finland, in the extreme northwest, are of a distinctly different race. In both these regions there were set up independent governments which resisted the rule of the Bolsheviki. With the aid of German troops the power of the Bolsheviki in the new states was soon destroyed. Through the setting up of these states, particularly Ukrainia, Germany hoped to secure grain supplies, and to control large iron and coal deposits. Dissatisfaction of the people with German control, however, interfered seriously with the realizing of such hopes.

TREATY OF BREST-LITOVSK
States and Provinces taken from Russia

The Peace of Brest-Litovsk. — On March 3 peace between Russia and the Central Powers was finally signed at Brest-Litovsk. By the terms of the treaties Russia was compelled (1) to surrender her western provinces of Poland, Lithuania, Livonia, Esthonia, and Courland; (2) to recognize the independence of Ukrainia and Finland; (3) to cede to Turkey certain important districts south of the Caucasus Mountains;[1] and (4) to pay a tremendous indemnity. The falsity of the German talk of "no annexations and no indemnities" was now evident. Few more disastrous treaties have ever been forced upon a vanquished nation. It has been estimated that the treaties of Brest-Litovsk took from Russia 4 per cent of her total area, 26 per cent of her population, 37 per cent of her food stuffs production, 26 per cent of her railways, 33 per cent of her manufacturing industries, 75 per cent of her coal, and 73 per cent of her iron.

Roumania Makes Peace. — Roumania, deserted by Russia, was forced to make peace in the spring of 1918, by ceding to her enemies the whole of the Dobrudja and also about 3000 square miles of territory on her western frontier. The Central Powers, moreover, were given control of the vast petroleum fields and the rich wheat lands of the defeated nation.

A little later, however, the Russian province of Bessarabia decided to unite itself to Roumania, as most of its people are of the Roumanian race.

The Russian Situation in 1918. — In spite of the Brest-Litovsk treaties, the Allies continued to regard Russia as a friendly nation. President Wilson took the lead in this attitude. It was felt that the Russian people were sadly in need of assistance, but just how this should be given was a serious problem.

[1] After driving the Russians out of Asia Minor and taking the districts ceded to Turkey, the Turkish forces went on and seized nearly all of the southern Caucasus before October, 1918.

The question was complicated by the presence in Russia of a large army of Czecho-Slovaks (check'o-slo-vaks'). These soldiers were natives of the northwestern Slavic provinces of Austria-Hungary. They had been part of the Austrian army during the victorious Russian campaigns in Galicia and had been taken prisoners. The Czecho-Slovaks had always sympathized with the Allied countries and had fought for Austria unwillingly. Many, indeed, had later fought as part of the Russian army. When Russia left the war they feared that they might be returned to the hated Austrian government. To avoid this their leaders sought and obtained from the Bolshevik government permission to travel eastward through Russia and Siberia to the Pacific. Here they planned to take ship and after a voyage three quarters around the globe take their place in the armies of the Allies. The long journey began. Then the Bolsheviki, probably acting under German orders, recalled the permission they had given. The Czecho-Slovaks went on nevertheless, determined to proceed even if they had to fight their way. They were opposed at different points by Bolshevik troops with the assistance of organized bodies of German and Austrian prisoners, but the Czecho-Slovaks were victorious. In fact, with the aid of anti-Bolshevik Russians they seized control of most of the Siberian railroad, and of parts of eastern Russia.

Allied Intervention in Russia.—At last the Allied nations and the United States decided that it was time to undertake military intervention in Russia. This was carried out in two places. Bodies of American and Japanese troops were landed on the east coast of Siberia to coöperate with the Czecho-Slovaks. The latter, thus reënforced, changed their plans for leaving Russia and decided to fight for the Allied cause where they were. They were encouraged by the fact that they were recognized by the Allies and by the United States as an independent nation.

Another small Allied army was landed on the north coast of Russia and marched south against the Bolsheviki. Large parts of Russia north and east of Moscow declared themselves free of Bolshevik rule. It was the hope of the Allies that that rule — now marked by pillage, murder, and famine — would shortly be overthrown and that a new Russia would rise and take its place among the democracies of the world.

The Western Front.—Early in 1918, after the failure of the German peace offensive in the west, rumors came from Germany of preparations for a great military drive on the western front. The "iron fist" and the "shining sword" were to break in the doors of those who opposed a German-made peace. There were good reasons for such an attack in the spring of 1918. Germany had withdrawn many troops from the east, where they were no longer needed to check the Russians. Further, although a few American troops had reached France, it was thought that not many could be sent over before the fall of 1918, and the full weight of

America's force could not be exerted before the summer of 1919. It was to Germany's interest to crush France and England before the power of the American nation was thrown into the struggle against her.

Germany's New Plan of Attack. — The German military leaders therefore determined to stake everything upon one grand offensive on the western front while their own force was numerically superior to that of the Allies. Their expectation of victory in what they proudly called the "Kaiser's battle," was based not only upon the possession of greater numbers, but also upon the introduction of new methods of fighting which would overcome the old trench warfare. The new methods comprised three principal features.

In the first place, much greater use was made of the element of surprise. Large masses of men were brought up near the front by night marches, and in daytime were hidden from airplane observation by smoke screens, camouflage of various kinds, and by the shelter of woodlands. In this way any portion of the opposing trench line could be subjected to a heavy, unexpected attack.

Secondly, the advance was prepared for by the use of big guns in enormous quantities and in new ways. The number of guns brought into use in this offensive far exceeded that put into the Verdun offensive of 1916, which had been looked upon as the extreme of possible concentration of artillery. The shell fire was now to be directed not only against the trenches, but also far to the rear of the Allied positions. This would break up roads, railways, and bridges for many miles behind the trenches and prevent the sending of reinforcements up to the front. Vast numbers of large shells containing poisonous "mustard" gas were collected. These were to be fired from heavy guns and made to explode far behind the Allied lines. By this means suffocation might be spread among the reserves, among motor drivers, and even among the army mules, and by deranging the transport service make it impossible to concentrate troops to withstand the German advance.

In the third place, "shock" troops composed of selected men from all divisions of the army, were to advance after the bombardment, in a series of "waves." When the first wave had reached the limit of its strength and endurance, it was to be followed up by a second mass of fresh troops, and this by a third, and so on until the Allies' defense was completely broken.

By their excess in numbers and by these newly devised methods of warfare the German leaders hoped to accomplish three things: (1) to separate the British army from the French army; (2) to seize the Channel ports and interrupt by submarines and big guns the transportation of men and supplies from England to France; and (3) to capture Paris and compel the French to withdraw from the war. Let us now see how and why the Germans failed to secure any one of these three objectives, and how the Allied forces resumed the offensive in the summer of 1918.

The German Advance.—Five great drives, conducted according to the newly devised methods of warfare, were launched by the Germans between March 21 and July 15, 1918. The first, continuing from March 21 to April 1, called the battle of Picardy, was directed at the point where the British army joined that of the French near the Somme River. There was at this time no unified command of all the Allied armies, and the blow fell unexpectedly upon the British and won much territory before French assistance could be brought up. Outnumbered three to one, the British fell back at the point of greatest retreat to a distance of thirty miles from their former line. But the extreme tenacity of the British and the arrival of French troops prevented the Germans from capturing the important city of Amiens (ah-myăn′), or reaching the main roads to Paris, or separating the British and French armies. Learning a needed lesson from this disaster, the Allied nations agreed to a unified military command, and appointed as commander-in-chief the French General Foch (fosh), who had distinguished himself in the first battle of the Marne in 1914 and elsewhere. Before this step had been taken General Pershing had offered his small army of 200,000 Americans to be used wherever needed by the French and the British.

The second German offensive began on April 9 and was again directed against the British, this time farther to the north, in Flanders, between the cities of Ypres and Arras. In ten days the Germans advanced to a maximum depth of ten miles on a front of thirty miles. But the British fought most desperately and the German losses were enormous. At last the advance was checked and the Channel ports were saved. "Germany on the march had encountered England at bay" — and had failed to destroy the heroic British army.

And now came a lull of over a month while the Germans were reorganizing their forces and preparing for a still greater blow. Again the element of surprise was employed. The Allies expected another attack somewhere in the line from Soissons to the sea, and their reserves were so disposed as to meet such an attack. But the German blow was directed against the weakest part of the Allied line, the stretch from Rheims to Soissons, where a break might open the road to Paris from the east. The third drive began on May 27. For over a week the French were pushed back, fighting valiantly, across land which had not seen the enemy since September, 1914. The greatest depth of the German advance was thirty miles, that is, to within forty-four miles of Paris. The enemy had once again reached the Marne River and controlled the main roads from Paris to Verdun and to the eastern parts of the Allied line.

The fourth drive started a few days later, on June 9, in a region where an attack was expected. It resulted in heavy losses to the Germans, who succeeded in pushing only six miles toward Paris in the region between Soissons and Montdidier (mawn-dee-dyā'). The advantages of a single command had begun to appear. General Foch could use all the Allied forces where they were most needed.

The fifth drive opened on July 15 and spread over a front of one hundred miles east of Soissons. The Allies were fully prepared, and while falling back a little at first, the American and French troops soon won back some of the abandoned territory.

The Turning of the Tide. — A glance at a map of the battle front of July 18 will show that the Germans had driven three blunt wedges into the Allied lines. These positions would prove dangerous to the Germans if ever the Allies were strong enough to assume the offensive. And just now the moment came for Foch to strike a great counter-blow. During the spring and early summer American troops had been speeded across the Atlantic until by the Fourth of July over a million men were in France. On July 18 fresh American and French troops attacked the Germans in the narrowest of the wedges along the Marne River and within a few days compelled the enemy to retreat from this wedge. On August 8 a British army began a surprise attack on the middle wedge, and by the use of large numbers of light, swift tanks succeeded in driving the Germans back for a distance of over ten miles on a wide front.

The offensive had now passed from the Germans to the Allies. Under Foch's repeated attacks the enemy was driven back first at one point and then at another. He had no time to prepare a counter-drive; he did not know where the next blow would fall. By the end of September he had given up nearly all his recent conquests, devastating much of the country as he retired. In several places also he was forced still farther back, across the old Hindenburg line. In two days (September 12–13) the Americans and French under the direction of General Pershing wiped out an old German salient near Metz, taking 200 square miles of territory and 15,000 prisoners. Altogether, by the end of September, Foch had taken over a quarter of a million prisoners, with 3,669 cannon and 23,000 machine guns.

It is said that the complete defeat of the German plans was due primarily to three things: "(1) the dogged steadfastness of the British and the patient heroism of the French soldiers and civilians; (2) the brilliant strategy of General Foch, and the unity of command which made this effective; (3) the material and moral encouragement of the American forces, of whom nearly 1,500,000 were in France before the end of August."

The War in Italy, the Balkans, and Syria. — The summer of 1918 witnessed the launching of a great offensive by the Austrians against the Italian armies holding the Piave front. It is probable that the chief purpose of this blow was to draw Allied troops into Italy from the battle front in Belgium and France. The Italians, however, proved themselves amply able to fight their own battle, and the Austrian attempt was repulsed with tremendous losses.

The autumn of this year saw important happenings on the Balkan front also. This theater of the war had been uneventful for a long time. The battle line extended from the Adriatic Sea to the Ægean, and was held by a mixed army of Serbians, Greeks, Italians, British, and French, under the command of General D'Esperey (des-prā'), with headquarters at Salonica. Opposed to these troops were armies of Bulgarians and Austrians, together with a considerable number of Germans. Encouraged by the German defeats in the west, which had forced the withdrawal of large numbers of German troops from eastern Europe, the Allies launched a strong offensive on the Balkan front in the middle of September. Day after day their advance continued, resulting in the capture of many thousands of prisoners and the reoccupation of many miles of Albanian and Serbian territory. The campaign was one of the most successful of the whole war. Within two weeks the Bulgarians asked for an armistice, accepted the terms that were demanded, and on September 30 definitely withdrew from the war. Their surrender broke the lines of communication between the Central Powers and Turkey and at one blow destroyed Teutonic supremacy in the Balkans. An even more important consequence was the moral effect on the general public in Germany, Austria, and Turkey, where it was taken by many as a sign that surrender of the Central Powers could only be a question of time.

Meanwhile, events of almost equal importance were taking place in Palestine and Syria. General Allenby had taken Jerusalem in December, 1917. In the fall of 1918 new and important advances were made in this region, Arab forces east of the Jordan coöperating with the British armies. By the close of September more than 50,000 Turkish soldiers and hundreds of guns had been captured. In October General Allenby's men took the important cities of Damascus and Aleppo, and in Mesopotamia also the British began a new advance. Turkey was already asking for an armistice, and now accepted terms that were virtually a complete surrender (October 31).

By this time Austria-Hungary was in the throes of dissolution; independent republics were being set up by the Czechs, the Hungarians, the Jugo-Slavs, and even the German Austrians. These revolutions were hastened by the overwhelming victory of the Italians in the second battle of the Piave. Their attack began October 24 on the mountain front, but soon the Allied forces under General Diaz (dee′ahss) crossed the river and cut through the lines of the fleeing Austrians. In the capture of large numbers of prisoners and guns the Italians took full vengeance for their defeat of the preceding year. So hopeless, indeed, was the situation for the Austrians that they too accepted an armistice that was practically a surrender (November 4).

German Retreat in the West. — After the Germans had been driven back to their old lines in France, there was danger that the contest might settle down to the old form of trench warfare. But the intricate defenses of the Hindenburg line, in some cases extending to a depth of ten miles from the front trenches, did not prove strong enough to withstand the American and Allied advance. Foch attacked the line from each end and also in the center. In the north, by October 20, Belgian and British troops had recaptured all the Belgian coast, with its submarine bases; and the British had taken the important cities of Lens and Lille, the former valuable on account of its coal mines. In the center British and French troops broke through to the important points of Cambrai, St. Quentin (săn-kahn-tăn') and Laon (lahn), while farther east the French and Americans began an advance along the Meuse River, threatening to attack the German line in the rear.

By this time it seemed likely that a general retirement from Belgium and France had been determined upon by the German leaders. Moreover, the impending defeat of the German armies led to a new peace drive by the German government. On October 6 President Wilson received a note from the German Chancellor asking for an armistice, requesting that the United States take steps for the restoration of peace, and stating that the German government accepted as a basis for peace negotiations the program as laid down in the President's message to Congress of January 8, 1918 (Chapter XIV), and in his subsequent addresses. In the ensuing correspondence several points are worthy of special notice. President Wilson opposed any suggestion of an armistice till after the evacuation of Allied territory, or except as it might be arranged by the military advisers of the American and Allied powers, on such terms as would make impossible the renewal of hostilities by Germany. He also called attention to the following point in his address of July 4, 1918,— "The destruction of every arbitrary power anywhere that can separately, secretly, and of its single choice disturb the peace of the world, or, if it cannot be presently destroyed, at the least its reduction to virtual impotence";—stated that the military autocracy still in control of Germany was such a power; and insisted on dealing only with a new or altered German government in which the representatives of the people should be the real rulers.

On November 11, while the German armies in France and Belgium were being defeated by the Allied and American forces, envoys from the German government accepted from General Foch an armistice in terms that meant virtually the surrender of Germany, and thus brought hostilities to an end.

Suggestions for Study. — 1. What is the meaning of camouflage? of smoke screen? What is a convoy? 2. On a map of the Western Front locate the five great German drives of 1918, numbering them from one to five. 3. On a physical map of the Balkan peninsula find the only good land route from the Danube to Constantinople, with its branch to Salonica. 4. Collect pictures showing American soldiers in camps; going to France; and in France. 5. What were the objects of the 1918 offensive of the Germans? 6. In what way did the American troops help besides increasing the number of soldiers fighting the Germans? 7. What is the present condition of the western provinces of Russia? 8. What was the first important battle in which many American troops were engaged? 9. Why was the St. Mihiel salient important: (*a*) for the Germans to hold; (*b*) for the Allies and the United States to win? 10. Explain the importance of Bulgaria's surrender.

References. — *War Cyclopedia* (C. P. I.); *The Study of the Great War* (C. P. I.); McKinley, *Collected Materials for the Study of the War; The Correspondence between the Bolsheviki and the German Government* (C. P. I.); *National School Service*, Vol. I (C. P. I.).

CHAPTER XIII

THE UNITED STATES IN THE WAR

Part of the Navy Sent to Europe. — One of the first things done after our entrance into the war was to send a considerable part of our navy to Europe, not only battleships to augment the fleet that was holding the German navy in check, but also a number of swift torpedo boats and destroyers to aid in reducing the menace from submarines. Huge appropriations were made by Congress for the purpose of increasing the number of lighter craft in the navy. Particularly efficient submarine chasers were developed, called "Eagles," which, by being made all alike, could be quickly produced in great numbers.

Raising the Army. — Great numbers of young men at once enlisted in various branches of the service. Profiting, however, by the experience of Great Britain, the government determined on conscription as a more democratic method of raising an army. A draft law was passed providing for the enrollment of all men between the ages of twenty-one and thirty-one. These were examined and classified, and from time to time large groups were sent to camps to be trained. Each of these camps can take care of approximately fifty thousand soldiers. Under a later draft law passed in 1918, the age limits for enrolling men were extended to include those from eighteen to forty-five.

Officers' Training Camps.—In order to provide officers for such an emergency as now confronted the nation, training camps for officers had been established the previous year at several places in the country. These officers were now called upon to aid the regular army officers in training the recruits. The officers' training camps have been continued and increased in number in order that a regular supply of properly trained officers may be available for the constantly increasing army.

Supplies and Munitions. — The industries of the country were compelled to turn their attention to the making of supplies and munitions for our fighters. The great plants that had been making powder, guns, shells, and other munitions for the Allies started to make these things for the United States. This was easy to arrange, since England and France had about reached a position where they were able to supply themselves. Besides, great quantities of food and clothing were also needed, and the meat packers and the manufacturers of textiles, shoes, and other articles turned their plants to the production of supplies for the army.

Aircraft. — The war in Europe had shown the high usefulness of aircraft as part of the military forces. Recognizing this, Congress appropriated two thirds of a billion dollars for the purpose of constructing thousands of airplanes and for training thousands of pilots and other experts to use them. Unfortunately much time was lost in building manufacturing plants and in experimenting with various types of engines and other parts of airplanes. Only a small part of the twenty thousand it had been planned to send to France by June, 1918, were completed at that time. Meanwhile, however, engineers had developed, on the basis of the automobile engine, an improved engine known as the Liberty Motor, and the production of efficient airplanes was at last going ahead rapidly.

Food and Fuel Control. — So large a proportion of the population of the European countries is employed in carrying on the war that there has been a constant decrease in the amount of food produced in Europe. Fortunately, up to 1917 this country had enough for itself and sufficient to spare for the Allies and the neutral nations. In 1917 there was an unusually short cereal crop all over the world. The result was that there was not enough food to go round, if every one in this country ate as much as usual.

In order that proper conservation of food might be brought about, a food commission was created, not only to prevent profiteering, but also to direct how the people should economize in order to help win the war. Shortages in various kinds of food were controlled at first through voluntary rationing under requests made by the Food Administrator. Later on, limits were placed on the amount of wheat, flour, and sugar that could be bought by large dealers and bakeries. A certain proportion of other cereals had to be purchased with each purchase of wheat. Bakers were required to make their bread with a proportion of other flours mixed with the wheat. These regulations were enforced by such punishments as fines, the closing of stores or bakeries, or by depriving the offender of his supply for a given length of time. Kitchens were established in large communities where housewives could learn the best ways of making bread with the use of various substitutes for wheat.

Early in the fall of 1917 it was seen that, because of inadequate transportation facilities and of a tremendously increasing demand for coal by the war industries, there would be a shortage of fuel during the winter. Accordingly a Fuel Administrator was appointed who regulated the distribution of fuel. Industries essential to the war were supplied, while those that were not doing needful work had their supply reduced or cut off altogether. As it happened, the winter of 1917–1918 was exceedingly severe, freight congestion became worse and worse, and the shortage in the industrial centers was even greater than had been anticipated. The control of fuel saved the people of the northeastern section of our country from much distress, and assured a supply of fuel for war purposes.

Later in 1918 householders and mercantile establishments were allowed only a portion of their usual coal supply, the number of stops made by street railway cars was reduced, and window and other display lighting was forbidden on all but two nights in the week. An act of Congress directed that from the last Sunday in March till the last Sunday in October all clocks must be set one hour ahead of time. This regulation brings more of our activities into the daylight hours and so cuts down the use of artificial light. By these methods much coal was conserved for the use of factories engaged in war work.

Transportation Control. — Soon after war was declared, the railroads of the country put themselves at the disposal of the government in order to take care of the increase in transportation service required by the state of war. The nearly seven hundred railroads of the country were organized and run as a single system under the direction of a Railroads' War Board, composed of some of the chief railroad officials.

Passenger train service was reduced, chiefly in order to provide for the transportation of several million soldiers to and from training camps. Freight cars and locomotives from one railroad were kept as long as they were needed in the service of another. The roads no longer competed with each other for freight, but goods were sent over the road that had, at the time of shipment, the most room for additional traffic. At the end of 1917, as a measure of economy and to secure even greater unity of organization, the government took over the control of the railroads for the period of the war. As Director General of Railroads, the President appointed William G. McAdoo, who was also the Secretary of the Treasury.

Half a year later, the government likewise took over,

for the duration of the war, the operation of telegraph and telephone lines, which were placed under the control of the Postmaster-General.

Shipbuilding. — Less than two weeks after the declaration of war the United States Shipping Board Emergency Fleet Corporation was organized with a capital of fifty million dollars all owned by the government. The Shipping Board had been formed some time before to increase the merchant shipping of the country. When war came, more and yet more ships were needed, not only to take our armies, and their food and fighting material, to Europe, but also to replace the shipping destroyed by submarines. In order that these ships might be built as speedily as possible it was desirable that the government should direct the work. Existing shipyards were taken over, and new shipyards were built by the government. In the building of ships the original program was more than doubled, and the United States became the greatest shipbuilding nation of the world. This was made possible largely through the construction of what are known as "fabricated ships"; that is, many ships built exactly alike, from parts made in quantities. Patterns are made for each special piece of steel and sent to steel plants in different parts of the country. There dozens of pieces are made exactly like the pattern. All the pieces for a ship are sent to the shipyard ready to be riveted in their proper places. Thus the shipyard can work much faster than if the pieces were prepared at the yard.

German Shipping Seized. — Immediately upon the declaration of war, the President ordered the seizure of ninety-nine German merchant ships which were in our ports. Most of them had been in harbor since August, 1914. They had been free to sail if they wished, but preferred not to risk capture by British or French warships.

When the United States officials took charge of these vessels, it was found that important parts of their machinery had been destroyed or broken, under orders from Germany. Repairs were quickly and skillfully made, the German names of the ships were changed, and a few months later over six hundred thousand tons of German-built ships were taking American troops and supplies across the seas.

Paying for the War. — Wars nowadays cost enormous sums of money, on account of the highly technical material that is used as well as the great size of the armies. There are two ways by which the money can be raised. The government can borrow money, and it can raise money by taxation. It was found wise to pay for the war by depending on both of these methods.

In May and June our people were called upon to subscribe to an issue of two billion dollars' worth of Liberty bonds. Half as much more was offered to the government. A second loan for three billions in November was again oversubscribed by fifty per cent. In 1918 the third loan for three billion, and the fourth loan, for six billion, were also oversubscribed. Up to November,

1918, the government asked for fourteen billion dollars, the people offered to lend about eighteen billion dollars, and the government accepted about sixteen billion dollars.

In addition to the above, the Treasury department authorized the sale of two billion dollars' worth of War Savings Stamps during the year 1918. These stamps represent short-time loans to the government which are so small that practically every person is able to invest in them.

It was deemed important also that the people should pay a large percentage of the war bill through taxes. Congress therefore passed a tax bill which not only increased the income taxes to be paid by individuals and companies, but also placed heavy taxes on many things which were more or less in the nature of luxuries, or at least were not essential to life. Railroad tickets, admission tickets to amusements of all sorts, telephone and telegraph messages, and hundreds of other things above a certain low minimum cost were taxed. In this way the government raised six or seven billion dollars in a single year, approximately one third of the current cost of the war.

Loans to the Allies. — Our government has from time to time advanced much money to the other nations who are fighting Germany. Practically all of these loans are in the form of credits with which the Allies pay for materials bought in the United States. Little if any of the money so loaned goes out of the country.

Red Cross and Other Organizations. — The American Red Cross Society, formed for the relief of suffering through war or other disaster, was made ready for extensive work by the subscription of one hundred and fifty million dollars in June, 1917, by the people of the country. The work was organized on a national basis and in every community there was formed a Red Cross Chapter to make garments, sweaters, or woolen head coverings to keep the soldiers warm; to roll bandages; to open canteens or refreshment stations for soldiers while traveling or in camp; to train nurses to care for the sick and wounded, and to do other work of a similar sort.

Other organizations such as the Young Men's Christian Association and the Knights of Columbus took upon themselves the task of entertaining and making comfortable our soldiers and sailors, providing places where they may read, write letters, play games, and otherwise relieve their minds from the terrible strain of war.

If our army and navy that are fighting for us in Europe represent the strength of our country, we can also say that the work of the Red Cross and these other organizations represents the heart of our country.

The Work of Schools in the War. — School pupils are the largest and best-organized group of the population of the country. It was natural, therefore, for the government to turn to the school children when it wanted a national response. Boys and girls having the lessons of the war impressed upon them in school, carry the message home. Often in no other way can the parents be reached.

There are many ways in which the school children gave direct and valuable help to the nation. It is not possible to do more than merely hint at some of these.

The importance of saving and thrift was early impressed on the children, not only through the thrift stamp and Liberty loan campaigns, but also through direct lessons on conserving food, clothing, and public and private property.

Many children planted and took care of war gardens, adding a total of many million dollars' worth of food to the nation's supply. In connection with the gardens, a canning campaign was conducted which aimed at the conservation of perishable food that could not be consumed at once.

The schools rendered valuable service in doing Red Cross work. Both boys and girls knit garments and comforts for our soldiers, and the girls made garments for the little children of France and Belgium who had been driven from their homes by the war.

Rise in Prices. — When a country is at war the government must have what it needs, quickly and at any price. The price situation is made worse if for any reason there happens to be a scarcity of a given article. When the government wants a great quantity of ammunition for which it is willing to pay a high price, the manufacturer, desiring to obtain an increased number of workmen quickly, offers unusually high pay. This attracts workmen from other industries, and the latter offer still higher pay to retain their workmen. In this way, wages rapidly go up and things that have to be produced with labor, like coal, or houses, or ships, rise enormously in cost. The farmer, too, has to pay more for his help. In order to induce the farmers to plant more wheat, the government fixed a high price for it. This helped to make flour expensive. Many fishermen went into the navy, or into factories where they could get high wages. If they kept on fishing, they thought they ought to make as much money as the men who had given up fishing and gone to make guns and build ships.

Perhaps the biggest reason for high prices is the actual scarcity of many things. Many of the men who do the work of producing are at war. They are using food and clothing much faster than if they were not soldiers. A soldier needs about twice as much food, and wears out eight times as many pairs of shoes, as he did when he was at home. From these facts it is easy to see why prices are high during the war.

Our Achievements in 1917.—As a result of our unwillingness, before 1917, to face the fact that we might sometime be involved in war, the tremendous amount of preparation described in this chapter had to be done in a few months, or even in a few weeks. When things have to be done in such a great hurry, missteps are often made and unfortunate delays result.

In spite of all difficulties, however, the United States had, at the end of 1917, two hundred and fifty thousand troops in France and a million and a half in training camps. Guns, rifles, clothing, shoes, food, and other necessary supplies were being produced in sufficient quantities. On the other side of the Atlantic, our engineers and railroad men were busy constructing docks, warehouses, and miles of railroad for the purpose of providing bases of supplies for our soldiers in France. Much of the equipment of these railroads and docks — cars, locomotives, and unloading machinery — had been brought from America.

More Soldiers Sent to France. — As the troops in the various camps and cantonments were trained they were sent to ports on the eastern coast and embarked for France, their places in camp being taken by new groups of drafted men. Beginning with fifty or sixty thousand each month, the number sent abroad was rapidly increased until by the fall of 1918 the troops were going over at the rate of more than three hundred thousand a month. By October 15 there were over two million of our soldiers in France and another million and more under training in this country.

Decrease in Submarine Sinkings. — The Germans had boasted in vain that their submarines would prevent the transportation of American troops to Europe. Of the hundreds of transports engaged in this work, up to November, 1918, only two were sunk while on the eastward voyage, and less than 300 American soldiers were drowned. Moreover, during the year 1918 there was a notable decrease in the destruction of merchant vessels by submarines. This was due probably to a variety of causes, but especially to the increased protection provided by the convoy system, and to the more efficient methods of fighting the submarines.

It has been found that it is possible to see a submarine at some distance below the surface if the observer is in a balloon or an airplane. Therefore the submarine hunters do not need to wait for the submarine to show itself. The sea is patrolled by balloons and airplanes in conjunction with fast destroyers. When the aircraft has located a submarine, the fact is signaled to a destroyer. When the destroyer arrives over the submarine, it drops a depth bomb, which is arranged to explode after it has sunk to any desired depth in the water.

It is believed that the submarines are being destroyed faster than Germany can build them, and also that it is increasingly difficult for Germany to obtain the highly trained crews necessary to manage the complex machinery of a submarine. For it must be remembered that the circumstances under which submarines are destroyed almost always involve the loss of the crew.

Submarines Raid the Atlantic Coast. — Unable to face the convoys of transports, several submarines paid visits to our coast in the summer of 1918, and destroyed a considerable number of unarmed vessels, mostly small craft. Many of the victims, indeed, were very small fishing boats, which are, by international agreement, exempt from capture or destruction.

German Propaganda. — Before the United States entered the war, our people were divided in their sympathies between the Central Powers and the Allies. Those who believed that Germany was right were chiefly people of German birth or descent, though a large majority even of this group did not believe in the things for which Germany was fighting.

Since the United States was neutral, their attitude was perfectly legal, provided their sympathies did not lead them to commit crimes against the United States in their zeal to hinder the cause of the Allies. Unfortunately, ever since we entered the war some of these people, still keeping on the side of Germany, have endeavored in every way to prevent the success of the American cause. Some of these men and women are American-born, others have, through naturalization, sworn to uphold the government of the United States, but still others have remained subjects of the Central Powers. They have organized plots either to destroy property, or to spread rumors intended to interfere with the prosecution of the war and to undermine confidence in the government.

Munition factories have been blown up, and information has been secretly sent to German authorities concerning the movements of ships so that they could be attacked by submarines. Worse than all else, perhaps, is the circulation of groundless rumors such as those stating that the soldiers have insufficient food or clothing, or insinuating that officers of the government are guilty of outrageous offenses in their treatment of men and women who have entered war service.

The Citizen and the Propagandist. — It is the duty of every true citizen, boy or girl, man or woman, to do two things to stop this treason talk. First, when some one tells you a thing about our government that ought not to be true, and sounds as if the speaker was trying to undermine the efforts of our country to win the war, ask him, "How do you know?" and then report the matter to the first policeman or other trustworthy person that you meet. The second thing you should do is carefully to avoid spreading any such rumors that you may hear.

How the Government Controls Propaganda. — Our country has sought to control the treasonable work of these propagandists in three ways.

First, all who are subjects of any enemy country, and who are above fourteen years of age, must be enrolled, and must carry a certificate with them wherever they go. They may not live within a half mile of navy yards, arsenals, or other places where war work is going on, and they may not go within three hundred feet of any wharf or dock.

Secondly, those whose conduct has been suspicious, or who have displayed active sympathy with the enemy in speech or act, as well as certain persons who were in official relationship with Germany, are interned for the duration of the war. Internment means that they are under close guard in a camp, or in a small district, but otherwise have considerable freedom.

In the third place, German sympathizers who have committed or have attempted to commit crimes endangering the lives of our citizens, or interfering in any way with the conduct of the war, have been sent to prison for long terms.

Suggestions for Study. — 1. Define cantonment; camp; barracks; army post. Describe the insignia of different grades of officers in the army and in the navy. Find some fact about General Pershing; about Admiral Sims. What is meant by propaganda? What is an alien enemy? 2. On a map of the United States mark the chief camps and cantonments. Locate the chief shipbuilding centers. 3. Make a collection of Food Saving notices and of literature and posters about Liberty Loans and War Savings Stamps. Make copies with names and dates of interesting letters from the front. 4. Collect pictures of shipbuilding and of transporting food to Europe. 5. Why did the navy go first to Europe? 6. How does the draft put a man into the army? 7. What factories near your home have done war work? 8. In what ways can a boy or girl save food? 9. Name five things on which you have to pay a war tax. 10. What can a boy or girl do for the Junior Red Cross? 11. Why do clothes and shoes cost more than before the war? 12. Why are some alien enemies put into prison or into detention camps?

References. — *National Service Handbook* (C. P. I.); *President's Flag Day Address with Evidence of Germany's Plans* (C. P. I.); Pamphlets from National Food Administrator; Pamphlets from National Fuel Administrator; *American Red Cross, Teachers Manual; German Plots and Intrigues* (C. P. I.); *Conquest and Kultur* (C. P. I.); the *World Almanac.*

CHAPTER XIV

QUESTIONS OF THE COMING PEACE

THERE are two kinds of problems which must be solved by the American people before permanent peace conditions can be established. One group of problems is composed of international questions, largely pertaining to the European states, but in which the United States is vitally interested. The other group of problems relates to the restoration of our people and industries to a peace condition. On some points these two groups of problems are closely related and cannot be settled separately. Some internal questions will have to be viewed in the light of world affairs; and some international problems must be given solutions which will have influences within our own country. Ignoring the overlapping of the two groups, we shall study the problems of peace in this chapter under two headings: (1) national problems; (2) international problems.

I. NATIONAL PROBLEMS

Among the many internal problems which the country will face at the close of the war, and to which every American should to-day be giving his earnest thought, the following are specially important.

Getting the Men Home. — Even while engaged in the task of getting every available man to the fighting line in Europe, the American authorities have found time to think of the return movement. It will be a great undertaking, requiring many months, to see that each man reaches American shores and after his dismissal is safely sent to his home town.

The Care of the Wounded. — During the war the greatest pains have been taken by the medical officers of the army, and by the Red Cross agents, to bring immediate relief to the brave wounded men, and to nurse them back to health. But many of them will have sacrificed an eye or a limb, or will have received wounds which will prevent their engaging in their previous occupations. It is the high duty of the nation to save such men from a life of pain or of enforced idleness. It should not permit them to subsist by charity, or even pensions. The wounded man, crippled for life in his nation's service, will be educated in a vocation which will occupy his mind, make him independent, and render him a respected and self-respecting member of his community. This great educational work has already been started, courses of study have been put into operation, and positions in various industrial plants have been guaranteed to the men after the training is completed. The nation will perform its whole duty to its heroes.

The Reconstruction of Industry. — The war has called into existence great plants for the manufacture of the specialties needed in warfare. Such factories must, after the close of the war, be made over and set to the task of creating goods for the days of peace. Machinery will be reconstructed, agencies for the sale of goods must be established, and foreign trade sought as a possible market for the enlarged production.

The Reorganization of Labor. — American working people, whether they be managers of plants or workmen at the machine, have been wonderfully loyal to the nation during the war. They have shifted their work, their homes, and their aspirations to meet the needs of the war. When peace returns all this talent and skill must be turned into other channels. This we hope can be accomplished without unemployment on a large scale, and without any loss of time or pay. But it will require great directing ability, and a friendly attitude of employees and employers toward each other.

Financial Reconstruction. — The finances of the government, of corporations, and of business men have been greatly changed during the course of the war. There may never be a complete return to the old conditions. But it is certain that peace will create problems of finance almost as serious as those of war.

Legislative Changes. — Our legislative bodies, particularly the Congress, will be called upon to pass many laws to aid the country to resume its peaceful life and occupations. All of the problems mentioned here, as well as many others, will require the enactment of new laws. We shall need congressmen and state legislators of wisdom, patriotism, and special knowledge to act intelligently for the people on these problems. The international settlements mentioned below also may require the action of the Senate upon treaties, and the action of both houses where laws are necessary to carry out our international agreements. The war has called for statesmanship of the highest order; the coming peace will make equal demands upon the wisdom and self-control of our statesmen and politicians.

II. International Problems

President Wilson, on January 8, 1918, addressed Congress in a speech which was designed to set forth the war aims and peace terms of the United States. Every American should be familiar with the terms of this "fourteen-point speech." Each one of the terms advocated by the President is given below in the President's own words, and a short explanatory paragraph is added to each.

1. *Open covenants of peace, openly arrived at, after which there shall be no private international understandings of any kind, but diplomacy shall proceed always frankly and in the public view.*

The President here speaks against the underhand diplomacy and secret alliances which have been a feature of European history in the past. By this practice a few diplomats and monarchs made whatever treaties they wished, not presenting them for ratification to the people's representatives, and yet binding every individual citizen to abide by the terms adopted. Such secret provisions have often been agreed to simply upon the whim or the ambition or the likes and dislikes of the rulers. They have sometimes been opposed to the true interests of the nations involved. They are undemocratic, and are not in accord with American ideas.

2. *Absolute freedom of navigation upon the seas, outside territorial waters, alike in peace and in war, except as the seas may be closed in whole or in part by international action for the enforcement of international covenants.*

Since 1793 the United States has stood for the freedom of the seas and the right of neutrals to carry on their trade in time of war as well as in time of peace. Germany's violation of our rights as a neutral by her submarine warfare was one of the causes of our taking up arms against her. By territorial waters the President here means the waters within three miles from shore, which are universally held to be under the complete control of the adjoining state. By international covenants are probably meant such covenants and guarantees as those mentioned in points 14, 1, 4, 11, 12, and 13.

3. *The removal, so far as possible, of all economic barriers and the establishment of an equality of trade conditions among all the nations consenting to the peace and associating themselves for its maintenance.*

Economic barriers are mainly restrictions upon trade and commerce. These restrictions take various forms; they may be prohibitive customs duties, or excessive port, tonnage, and harbor charges; they may be trade agreements granting favors to the citizens of one country and not to those of another. The President urges the establishment of an equality of such trade conditions.

4. *Adequate guarantees given and taken that national armaments will be reduced to the lowest point consistent with domestic safety.*

The President here touches one of the most important problems of the coming peace. This has often been called a war against war; it has been said that it will be the last war. The sentiment which leads to such statements has its origin in a hatred of militarism. Great armaments were created because of the danger from Prussian militarism; and great armaments will still be necessary unless "this intolerable thing" is crushed or "shut out from the friendly intercourse of the nations." When it is crushed, some adequate steps must be taken by each state to reduce its armaments, on condition that all other states do the same. But many problems will face the world's statesmen in preparing a plan for guaranteed disarmament. How large a force will each nation need to maintain its "domestic safety"? How shall we be sure that Germany will not break her promise, as she has so often done in this war? How shall we be sure that Germany, or perhaps some other state, will not again secretly prepare for a war while others remain unprepared?

5. *A free, open-minded, and absolutely impartial adjustment of all colonial claims, based upon a strict*

observance of the principle that in determining all such questions of sovereignty the interests of the populations concerned must have equal weight with the equitable claims of the government whose title is to be determined.

In the opening chapters of this book we have seen how colonial rivalry was one of the causes of the World War. The President urges that the settlement after the war shall be "free, open-minded, and absolutely impartial." He introduces here the democratic principle that the interests of the populations in the colonies shall have equal weight with the just claims of the European states. Such a principle probably will mean that few if any of Germany's colonies can be returned to her, because her colonial management has been neglectful of the interests of the subject peoples.

6. *The evacuation of all Russian territory and such a settlement of all questions affecting Russia as will secure the best and freest coöperation of the other nations of the world in obtaining for her an unhampered and unembarrassed opportunity for the independent determination of her own political development and national policy and assure her of a sincere welcome into the society of free nations under institutions of her own choosing, and, more than a welcome, assistance also of every kind that she may need and may herself desire. The treatment accorded Russia by her sister nations in the months to come will be the acid test of their good will, of their comprehension of her needs as distinguished from their own interests, and of their intelligent and unselfish sympathy.*

No restatement of the President's words on this subject is necessary. The Russian revolution is one of the most important results of the Great War. How can the future welfare of Russia be best secured?

7. *Belgium, the whole world will agree, must be evacuated and restored, without any attempt to limit the sovereignty which she enjoys in common with all other free nations. No other single act will serve as this will serve to restore confidence among the nations in the laws which they have themselves set and determined for the government of their relations with one another. Without this healing act the whole structure and validity of international law is forever impaired.*

The evacuation of Belgium will follow the military victories of the United States and her associates. The restoration of Belgium will be difficult to effect. It implies relief to her suffering and starving people, the return of the many exiles to Belgium, the erection of new homes for them, the reorganization of industry and transportation, and the repair and rebuilding of her historic edifices. Where will the funds come from for such work? Germany, the aggressor, surely should bear a part or all of the cost.

8. *All French territory should be freed and the invaded portions restored, and the wrong done to France by Prussia in 1871 in the matter of Alsace-Lorraine, which has unsettled the peace of the world for nearly fifty years, should be righted, in order that peace may once more be made secure in the interest of all.*

Here the President urges the same treatment for the occupied lands of northern France as for those of Belgium. The devastated lands must be reclaimed, the inhabitants cared for, and adequate means provided by which they can earn a livelihood. Further, he advises the return of Alsace-Lorraine to France. Such action not only will right the wrong done to France in 1871, but also it will take from Germany much of the iron-producing areas which have made it possible for her to prepare and carry on this war, and which might permit her to get ready for a yet more dreadful war in the future.

9. *A readjustment of the frontiers of Italy should be effected along clearly recognizable lines of nationality.*

We have seen how a considerable area inhabited by Italians was not freed from Austrian rule when the Italian kingdom was founded. This territory, called Italia Irredenta (unredeemed Italy), and this population, by its own desire and by natural right, belong to Italy and should be brought within the nation.

10. *The peoples of Austria-Hungary, whose place among the nations we wish to see safeguarded and assured, should be accorded the freest opportunity of autonomous development.*

Within the Austro-Hungarian boundaries are several nationalities which have been subjected to the oppressive rule of peoples different from themselves. Their attempts to obtain home rule or independence have been crushed. America now wishes to secure for these peoples the opportunity to establish governments for themselves. As we have already seen, our country in 1918 formally recognized the independence of one of these peoples — the Czecho-Slovaks, or inhabitants of Bohemia and neighboring districts. Moreover, in a note to Austria-Hungary, October 18, 1918, President Wilson stated that conditions had changed since January 8, and intimated that both the Czecho-Slovaks and the Jugo-Slavs should be given independence.

11. *Roumania, Serbia, and Montenegro should be evacuated, occupied territories restored, Serbia accorded free and secure access to the sea, and the relations of the several Balkan states to one another determined by friendly counsel along historically established lines of allegiance and nationality; and international guarantees of the political and economic independence and territorial integrity of the several Balkan states should be entered into.*

We have here a comprehensive plan for the settlement of the Balkan jealousies, which have disturbed Europe for many years. Evacuation and restoration is here proposed, as in Belgium and France. Serbia, always thwarted by Austria in her hopes for a port, is to be given access to the sea. Friendly counsel shall be given the Balkan peoples to aid them in establishing their governments along the lines of nationalities and of historic sympathies. All the countries of the world should unite to guarantee and protect the safety and independence of the governments established in the Balkan region.

12. *The Turkish portions of the present Ottoman Empire should be assured a secure sovereignty, but the other nationalities which are now under Turkish rule should be assured an undoubted security of life and an absolutely unmolested opportunity of autonomous development, and the Dardanelles should be permanently opened as a free passage to the ships and commerce of all nations under international guarantees.*

The horrible rule of the Turks over subject peoples must cease. The Turks, as well as all other peoples, should be allowed the right of self-government. But their subject peoples must also be protected in their lives, property, and occupations, and given an opportunity to establish self-government when they desire it. The Dardanelles strait must be taken out of the power of the Turks, and placed under the control of the associated nations.

13. *An independent Polish state should be erected which should include the territories inhabited by indisputably Polish populations, which should be assured a free and secure access to the sea, and whose political and economic independence and territorial integrity should be guaranteed by international covenant.*

A nation composed of Poles would imply the union of parts of Russia, Prussia, and Austria, since all of these three countries took part in the infamous partition of Poland in the eighteenth century. Access to the Baltic Sea would be necessary for the prosperity and independence of the new state. But such access could be gained only across territory which Prussia has held for a century and a half. The associated nations would guarantee the independence of Poland in the same way that they would protect Belgium, Serbia, and the other states erected upon the principle of national self-government.

14. *A general association of nations must be formed under specific covenants for the purpose of affording mutual guarantees of political independence and territorial integrity to great and small states alike.*

This is the most important of the President's suggestions. Without some form of a league of nations it will be impossible to adopt and carry out the other terms of the President's program. International guarantees, so frequently mentioned in his proposals, imply some means by which the countries of the world can act together for their common purposes. Restoration of devastated lands, disarmament, new democratic governments, freedom of commerce, — all of these things will remain nothing but rainbow hopes unless the large and small nations of the world unite for their realization. A League of Nations, more or less regularly organized, must be formed if the democracies of the world shall be made safe from future wars of aggression.

Suggestions for Study. — 1. Why are waters within three miles of shore considered as territorial waters? (See *War Cyclopedia*, "Marine League.") What is meant by freedom of the seas? What is meant by the phrase "free ships make free goods"?

2. Make a map of Europe showing what it would be like if all of President Wilson's points were approved at the peace conference. 3. Are there any reasons why every nation should give up its colonies and permit them to be independent states? 4. Why is it dangerous as well as wrong to permit Germany to retain her control over the territory taken from Russia? 5. What was the "wrong done to France (by Germany) in 1870"? 6. What is autonomy? Name the peoples of Austria-Hungary who wish autonomous development, or complete independence. 7. Find some ways by which Poland and Serbia can get access to the sea. 8. Do you think it will take a longer or a shorter time to bring the soldiers home than it did to send them to France? Why? 9. What is meant by rehabilitation of the wounded? Find some ways in which other nations have made their maimed soldiers self-supporting. 10. How is it likely that Constantinople will be controlled after the war? 11. How would the league of nations enforce its decisions? (See President Wilson's second point.)

References. — *War Cyclopedia* (C. P. I.); McKinley, *Collected Materials for the Study of the War; War, Labor, and Peace* (C. P. I.); *Conquest and Kultur* (C. P. I.); *The War Message and the Facts Behind It* (C. P. I.); *American Interest in Popular Government Abroad* (C. P. I.).

CHRONOLOGY — PRINCIPAL EVENTS OF THE WAR

(Adapted from "War Cyclopedia" published by the Committee on Public Information, Washington, D. C. Events which especially concern the United States are put in *italic* type.)

1914

June 28 Murder of Archduke Francis Ferdinand at Serajevo.
July 5 Conference at Potsdam (page 70).
July 23 Austro-Hungarian ultimatum to Serbia.
July 28 Austria-Hungary declares war on Serbia.
July 31 German ultimatums to Russia and France.
Aug. 1 Germany declares war on Russia and invades Luxemburg.
Aug. 2 German ultimatum to Belgium, demanding a free passage for her troops across Belgium.
Aug. 3 Germany declares war on France.
Aug. 4–26 Most of Belgium overrun: Liege occupied (Aug. 9); Brussels (Aug. 20); Namur (Aug. 24).
Aug. 4 Great Britain declares war on Germany.
Aug. 4 President Wilson proclaims neutrality of United States.
Aug. 6 Austria-Hungary declares war on Russia.
Aug. 12 France and Great Britain declare war on Austria-Hungary
Aug. 16 British expeditionary force landed in France.
Aug. 18 Russia invades East Prussia.
Aug. 21–23 Battle of Mons-Charleroi. Dogged retreat of French and British in the face of the German invasion.
Aug. 23 Japan declares war on Germany.
Aug. 23 Tsingtau (Kiaochow) bombarded by Japanese.
Aug. 25–Dec. 15 Russians overrun Galicia. Lemberg taken (Sept. 2); Przemysl besieged (Sept. 16 to Oct. 15, and again after Nov. 12). Dec. 4, Russians 3½ miles from Cracow.
Aug. 26 Germans destroy Louvain, in Belgium.
Aug. 26 Allies conquer Togo, in Africa.
Aug. 26–31 Russians defeated in battle of Tannenberg (page 85).
Aug. 28 British naval victory of Helgoland Bight, in North Sea.
Aug. 31 Name of St. Petersburg changed to Petrograd.
Sept. 5 Great Britain, France, and Russia agree not to make peace separately.

Sept. 6–10 First battle of the Marne (page 81).
Sept. 7 Germans take Maubeuge, in northern France.
Sept. 11 Australians take German New Guinea, etc.
Sept. 12–17 Battle of the Aisne.
Sept. 16 Russians driven from East Prussia.
Sept. 22 Three British armored cruisers sunk by a submarine.
Sept. 27 Invasion of German Southwest Africa by Gen. Botha.
Oct. 9 Germans occupy Antwerp, the chief port of Belgium.
Oct. 16–28 Battle of the Yser, in Flanders, Belgium. Belgians and French halt German advance.
Oct. 17–Nov. 15 Battle of Flanders, near Ypres, saving Channel ports.
Oct. 21–28 German armies driven back in Poland.
Oct. 28–Dec. 8 De Wet's rebellion in British South Africa.
Oct. 29 Turkish war ship bombards Odessa, Russia.
Nov. 1 German naval victory off the coast of Chile.
Nov. 3–5 Russia, France, and Great Britain declare war on Turkey.
Nov. 7 Fall of Tsingtau (Kiaochow) to the Japanese and British.
Nov. 10–Dec. 14 Austrian invasion of Serbia (page 87).
Nov. 10 German cruiser "Emden" destroyed in Indian Ocean.
Nov. 21 Basra, on Persian Gulf, occupied by British.
Dec. 8 British naval victory off the Falkland Islands.
Dec. 16 German warships bombard towns on east coast of England.
Dec. 17 Egypt proclaimed a British protectorate, under a sultan.
Dec. 24 First German air raid on England.

1915

Jan. 1–Feb. 15 Russians attempt to cross the Carpathians.
Jan. 24 British naval victory of Dogger Bank, in North Sea.
Jan. 25–Feb. 12 Russians again invade East Prussia, but are defeated in the battle of the Mazurian Lakes.
Jan. 28 American merchantman "William P. Frye" sunk by German cruiser.
Feb. 4 Germany's proclamation of "war zone" around the British Isles after February 18.
Feb. 10 United States note holding German government to a "strict accountability" for destruction of American lives or vessels.
Feb. 19 Anglo-French squadron bombards Dardanelles forts.
Mar. 1 Announcement of British "blockade" of Germany.
Mar. 10 British capture Neuve Chapelle, in northern France.
Mar. 22 Russians capture Przemysl, in Galicia.
Apr. 17–May 17 Battle of Ypres. First use of poison gas (page 95).
Apr. 25 Allied troops land on the Gallipoli peninsula.
Apr. 30 Germans invade the Baltic provinces of Russia.
May 1 American steamship "Gulflight" sunk by German submarine; two Americans lost.

May 2 Battle of the Dunajec. Russians defeated by the Germans and Austrians and forced to retire from the Carpathians.

May 7 British liner "Lusitania" sunk by German submarine (1,154 lives lost, *114 being Americans*).

May 9–June Battle of Artois, or Festubert (in France, north of Arras). Small gains by the Allies.

May 13 American note protests against submarine policy culminating in the sinking of the "Lusitania." Other notes June 9, July 21; German replies, May 28, July 8, Sept. 1.

May 23 Italy declares war on Austria-Hungary.

May 25 American steamship "Nebraskan" attacked by submarine.

June 3 Przemysl retaken by Germans and Austrians.

June 9 Monfalcone occupied by Italians.

June 22 The Austro-Germans recapture Lemberg, in Galicia.

July 2 Naval action between Russians and Germans in the Baltic.

July 9 Conquest of German Southwest Africa completed.

July 12–Sept. 18 German conquest of Russian Poland; capture of Warsaw (Aug. 5), Kovno (Aug. 17), Brest-Litovsk (Aug. 25), Vilna (Sept. 18).

Aug. 19 British liner "Arabic" sunk by submarines (44 victims, *two Americans*).

Aug. 21 Italy declares war on Turkey.

Sept. 1 The German ambassador, von Bernstorff, gives assurance that German submarines will sink no more liners without warning.

Sept. 8 United States demands recall of Austro-Hungarian ambassador, Dr. Dumba.

Sept. 25–Oct. French offensive in Champagne fails to break through German lines.

Sept. 27 Small British progress at Loos, near Lens.

Oct. 4 Russian ultimatum to Bulgaria.

Oct. 5 Allied forces land at Salonica, at the invitation of the Greek government.

Oct. 5 German Government regrets and disavows sinking of "Arabic" and is prepared to pay indemnities.

Oct. 6–Dec. 2 Austro-German-Bulgarian conquest of Serbia; fall of Belgrade (Oct. 9), Nish (Nov. 1), Monastir (Dec. 2).

Oct. 13 Germans execute the English nurse, Edith Cavell, for aiding Belgians to escape from Belgium.

Oct. 14 Bulgaria declares war on Serbia.

Oct. 15–19 Great Britain, France, Russia, and Italy declare war against Bulgaria.

Nov. 10–Apr. Russian forces advance into Persia as a result of pro-German activities there.

Dec. 1 British under Gen. Townshend retreat from near Bagdad to Kut-el-Amara.

Dec. 3 United States Government demands recall of Capt. Boy-Ed and Capt. von Papen, attachés of the German embassy.

Dec. 6 Germans capture Ipek, in Montenegro.
Dec. 15 Sir Douglas Haig succeeds Sir John French in command of the British army in France.
Dec. 19 British forces withdraw from parts of Gallipoli peninsula.

1916

Jan. 8 Evacuation of Gallipoli completed.
Jan. 13 Fall of Cetinje, capital of Montenegro.
Feb. 10 Germany notifies neutral powers that armed merchant ships will be treated as warships and will be sunk without warning.
Feb. 15 Secretary Lansing states that by international law commercial vessels have right to carry arms in self-defense.
Feb. 16 Germany sends note acknowledging her liability in the "Lusitania" affair.
Feb. 16 Russians take Erzerum, in Turkish Armenia.
Feb. 16 Kamerun (Africa) conquered.
Feb. 21–July Battle of Verdun (pages 107–108).
Feb. 24 President Wilson in letter to Senator Stone refuses to advise American citizens not to travel on armed merchant ships.
Mar. 8 Germany declares war on Portugal.
Mar. 24 French steamer "Sussex" is torpedoed without warning (page 115).
Apr. 18 Russians capture Trebizond, in Turkey.
Apr. 18 United States note declaring that she will sever diplomatic relations unless Germany abandons present methods of submarine warfare.
Apr. 24–May 1 Insurrection in Ireland.
Apr. 29 Gen. Townshend surrenders at Kut-el-Amara.
May 4 Germany's conditional pledge not to sink merchant ships without warning (page 116).
May 14–June 3 Great Austrian attack on the Italians through the Trentino.
May 19 Russians join British on the Tigris.
May 24 Conscription bill becomes a law in Great Britain.
May 31 Naval battle off Jutland, in North Sea.
June 4–30 Russian offensive in Gâlicia and Bukowina.
June 5 Lord Kitchener drowned.
July 1–Nov. 17 Battle of the Somme (page 108).
July 27 Germans execute Captain Fryatt, an Englishman, for having defended his merchant ship by ramming the German submarine that was about to attack it.
Aug. 9 Italians capture Gorizia.
Aug. 27 Italy declares war on Germany.
Aug. 27–Jan. 15 Roumania enters war on the side of the Allies, and most of the country is overrun. (Fall of Bucharest, Dec. 6.)
Oct. 7 German submarine appears off American coast and sinks British passenger steamer "Stephano" (Oct. 8).
Nov. 19 Monastir retaken by Allies (chiefly Serbians).

Nov. 29 *United States protests against Belgian deportations.*
Dec. 6 Lloyd George succeeds Asquith as British prime minister.
Dec. 12 German peace offer. Refused (Dec. 30) as "empty and insincere."
Dec. 18 *President Wilson's peace note.* Germany replies evasively (Dec. 26). Entente Allies' reply (Jan. 10) demands "restorations, reparation, indemnities."

1917

Jan. 10 The Allied governments state their terms of peace.
Jan. 31 Germany announces unrestricted submarine warfare in specified zones.
Feb. 3 *United States severs diplomatic relations with Germany.*
Feb. 24 Kut-el-Amara taken by British under Gen. Maude.
Feb. 26 *President Wilson asks authority to arm merchant ships.*
Feb. 28 *"Zimmermann note" published.*
Mar. 11 Bagdad captured by British under Gen. Maude.
Mar. 11–15 Revolution in Russia, leading to abdication of Czar Nicholas II (Mar. 15). Provisional Government formed by Constitutional Democrats under Prince Lvov.
Mar. 12 *United States announces that an armed guard will be placed on all American merchant vessels sailing through the war zone.*
Mar. 17–19 Retirement of Germans to the "Hindenburg line" (page 118).
Mar. 24 *Minister Brand Whitlock and American Relief Commission withdrawn from Belgium.*
Apr. 2 *President Wilson asks Congress to declare the existence of a state of war with Germany.*
Apr. 6 *United States declares war on Germany.*
Apr. 8 *Austria-Hungary severs diplomatic relations with the United States.*
Apr. 9–May 14 British successes in battle of Arras (Vimy Ridge taken Apr. 9).
Apr. 16–May 6 French successes in battle of the Aisne between Soissons and Rheims.
Apr. 21 *Turkey severs relations with United States.*
May 4 *American destroyers begin coöperation with British navy in war zone.*
May 15–Sept. 15 Great Italian offensive on Isonzo front.
May 15 Gen. Pétain succeeds Gen. Nivelle as commander in chief of the French armies.
May 18 *President Wilson signs selective service act.*
June 7 British blow up Messines Ridge, south of Ypres, and capture 7,500 German prisoners.
June 10 Italian offensive in Trentino.
June 12 King Constantine of Greece forced to abdicate.
June 26 *First American troops reach France.*
June 29 Greece enters war against Germany and her allies.
July 1 Russian army led in person by Kerensky, the Minister of War, begins an offensive in Galicia, ending in disastrous retreat (July 19–Aug. 3).

July 20 Kerensky succeeds Prince Lvov as premier of Russia.

July 30 Mutiny in German fleet at Wilhelmshaven and Kiel. Second mutiny Sept. 2.

July 31–Nov. Battle of Flanders (Passchendaele Ridge); British successes.

Aug. 15 Peace proposals of Pope Benedict published (dated Aug. 1). *United States replies Aug. 27;* Germany and Austria, Sept. 21.

Aug. 15 Canadians capture Hill 70, dominating Lens.

Aug. 19–24 New Italian drive on the Isonzo front.

Aug. 20–24 French attacks at Verdun recapture high ground lost in 1916.

Sept. 3 Riga captured by Germans.

Sept. 8 Luxburg dispatches ("Spurlos versenkt") published by United States.

Sept. 15 Russia proclaimed a republic.

Oct. 17 Russians defeated in a naval engagement in the Gulf of Riga.

Oct. 14–Dec. Great German-Austrian invasion of Italy. Italian line shifted to Piave River.

Oct. 26 Brazil declares war on Germany.

Nov. 2 Germans retreat from the Chemin des Dames, in France.

Nov. 3 First clash of American with German soldiers.

Nov. 7 Overthrow of Kerensky and Provisional Government of Russia by the Bolsheviki.

Nov. 13 Clémenceau succeeds Ribot as French premier,

Nov. 20–Dec. 13 Battle of Cambrai (page 119).

Nov. 29 First plenary session of the Interallied Conference in Paris. Sixteen nations represented. *Col. E. M. House, chairman of American delegation.*

Dec. 3 Conquest of German East Africa completed.

Dec. 6 U. S. destroyer "Jacob Jones" sunk by submarine, with loss of over 60 American men.

Dec. 6 Explosion on munitions vessel wrecks Halifax.

Dec. 7 United States declares war on Austria-Hungary.

Dec. 10 Jerusalem captured by British.

Dec. 23 Peace negotiations opened at Brest-Litovsk between Bolshevik government and Central Powers.

Dec. 28 President Wilson takes over the control of railroads.

1918

Jan. 4 British hospital ship "Rewa" torpedoed and sunk in English Channel.

Jan. 8 President Wilson sets forth peace program of the United States.

Jan. 18 Russian Constituent Assembly meets in Petrograd.

Jan 19 The Bolsheviki dissolve the Russian Assembly.

Jan. 28 Revolution begins in Finland; fighting between "White Guards" and "Red Guards."

Jan. 28–29 Big German air raid on London.

Jan. 30 German air raid on Paris.

Feb. 3 *American troops officially announced to be on the Lorraine front near Toul.*

Feb. 5 British transport "Tuscania" with 2,179 American troops on board torpedoed and sunk; *211 American soldiers lost.*

Feb. 9 Ukrainia makes peace with Germany.

Feb. 10 The Bolsheviki order demobilization of the Russian army.

Feb. 14 Bolo Pasha condemned for treason against France; executed April 16.

Feb. 17 Cossack General Kaledines commits suicide. Collapse of Cossack revolt against the Bolsheviki.

Feb. 18–Mar. 3 Russo-German armistice declared at an end by Germany; war resumed. Germans occupy Dvinsk, Minsk, and other cities.

Feb. 21 German troops land in Finland.

Feb. 23 Turkish troops drive back the Russians in the northeast (Trebizond taken Feb. 26, Erzerum March 14).

Mar. 2 German and Ukrainian troops defeat the Bolsheviki near Kief in Ukrainia.

Mar. 3 Bolsheviki sign peace treaty with Germany at Brest-Litovsk. Ratified by Soviet Congress at Moscow March 15.

Mar. 7 Finland and Germany sign a treaty of peace.

Mar. 10 *Announcement that American troops are occupying trenches at four different points on French front.*

Mar. 11 *First wholly American raid, made in sector north of Toul, meets with success.*

Mar. 11 Great German air raid on Paris, by more than fifty planes.

Mar. 13 German troops occupy Odessa on Black Sea.

Mar. 21–Apr. 1 First German drive of the year, on 50-mile front, extending to Montdidier (page 143).

Apr. 9–18 Second German drive, on a 30-mile front between Ypres and Arras.

May 6 Roumania signs peace treaty with the Central Powers.

May 7 Nicaragua declares war on Germany and her allies.

May 9–10 British naval force attempts to block Ostend harbor.

May 14 Caucasus proclaims itself an independent state; but the Turks overrun the southern part, and take Baku Sept. 19.

May 21 British transport "Moldavia" is sunk *with loss of 53 American soldiers.*

May 24 *Major General March appointed Chief of Staff with the rank of General.*

May 24 Costa Rica declares war on the Central Powers.

May 25–June *German submarines appear off American coast and sink 19 coastwise vessels, including Porto Rico liner "Carolina" with loss of 16 lives.*

May 27–June 1 Third German drive, capturing the Chemin des Dames and reaching the Marne River east of Chateau-Thierry. *American Marines aid French at Chateau-Thierry.*

May 28 *American forces near Montdidier capture village of Cantigny and hold it against numerous counter-attacks.*

May 31 *U. S. transport "President Lincoln" sunk by U-boat while on her way to the United States; 23 lives lost.*

June 9–16 Fourth German drive, on 20-mile front east of Montdidier, makes only small gains.

June 10 Italian naval forces sink one Austrian dreadnaught and damage another in the Adriatic.

June 11 *American Marines take Belleau Wood, with 800 prisoners.*

June 14 Turkish troops occupy Tabriz, Persia.

June 15 *General March announces that there are 800,000 American troops in France.*

June 15–July 6 Austrian offensive against Italy fails with heavy losses.

June 21 *Official statement that American forces hold 39 miles of French front in six sectors.*

June 27 British hospital ship "Llandovery Castle" is torpedoed off Irish coast with loss of 234 lives. Only 24 survived.

July 10 Italians and French take Berat in Albania.

July 13 Czecho-Slovak troops occupy Irkutsk in Siberia.

July 15–18 *Anglo-American forces occupy strategic positions on the Murman Coast in northwestern Russia.*

July 15–18 Fifth German drive extends three miles south of the Marne, but east of Rheims makes no gain.

July 16 Ex-Czar Nicholas executed by Bolshevik authorities.

July 18–Aug. 4 Second battle of the Marne, beginning with Foch's counter-offensive between Soissons and Chateau-Thierry. French *and Americans* drive the Germans back from the Marne nearly to the Aisne.

July 22 Honduras declares war on Germany.

July 27 *American troops arrive on the Italian front.*

July 31 *President Wilson takes over telegraph and telephone systems.*

Aug. 2 Allies occupy Archangel, in northern Russia.

Aug. 8–Sept. Allies attack successfully near Montdidier, and continue the drive until the Germans are back at the Hindenburg line, giving up practically all the ground they had gained this year.

Aug. 15 *American troops land in eastern Siberia.*

Sept. 3 *The United States recognizes the Czecho-Slovak government.*

Sept. 12–13 *Americans take the St. Mihiel salient near Metz.*

Sept. 15 Allied army under Gen. D'Esperey begins campaign against Bulgarians.

Sept. 16 *President Wilson receives an Austrian proposal for a peace conference, and refuses it.*

Sept. 22 Great victory of British and Arabs over Turks in Palestine.

Sept. 26 *Americans begin a drive in the Meuse valley.*

Sept. 30 Bulgaria withdraws from the war.

Oct. 1 St. Quentin (on the Hindenburg line) taken by the French.

Oct. 1 Damascus captured by the British.

Oct. 3 King Ferdinand of Bulgaria abdicates.
Oct. 3 Lens taken by the British.
Oct. 4 *Germany asks President Wilson for an armistice and peace negotiations* (page 150); *other notes Oct. 12, 20, etc.; similar notes from Austria-Hungary Oct. 7, and from Turkey Oct. 12. Wilson's replies Oct. 8, 14, 18, 23.*
Oct. 7 Beirut taken by a French fleet.
Oct. 8 Cambrai taken by the British.
Oct. 13 Laon taken by the French.
Oct. 17 Ostend taken by the Belgians.
Oct. 17 Lille taken by the British.
Oct. 24–Nov. 4 Allied forces (chiefly Italians) under Gen. Diaz win a great victory on the Italian front.
Oct. 26 Aleppo taken by the British.
Oct. 31 Turkey surrenders.
Nov. 1 Serbian troops enter Belgrade after regaining nearly all of Serbia.
Nov. 3 Trieste and Trent occupied by Italian forces.
Nov. 4 Surrender of Austria-Hungary.
Nov. 5 *President Wilson notifies Germany that General Foch has been authorized by the United States and the Allies to communicate the terms of an armistice.*
Nov. 6 Mutiny of German sailors at Kiel; followed by mutinies, revolts, and revolutions at other German cities.
Nov. 7 Americans take Sedan.
Nov. 9 British take Maubeuge.
Nov. 9 Abdication of the German emperor William II and the crown prince; they flee to Holland Nov. 10.
Nov. 11 Armistice signed; Germany surrenders.

INDEX